Dear Victoria

I hope you enjoy reading this small memento of your time at Gresham's.

Wishing you every success and happiness in the future.

Philip John
Headmaster

GRESHAM'S

Howson of Holt

Olive Edis

G. W. S. HOWSON
1917

Howson of Holt

A Successful Radical in Education

by J. H. Simpson

Introduction by Hugh Wright and John Smart

Published by
Cambridge Occupational Analysts Ltd
for Gresham's School, Holt, Norfolk

Howson of Holt
This 2nd Edition published in 2010 by
Cambridge Occupational Analysts Ltd
for Gresham's School, Holt, Norfolk.

Introduction © Hugh Wright, John Smart

British Library Cataloguing in Publication Data
A catalogue record for this book is available from the British Library.
ISBN (hardback) 978-1-906711-09-2
ISBN (paperback) 978-1-906711-08-5

Printed in Great Britain by Page Brothers, Norwich, Norfolk.

CONTENTS

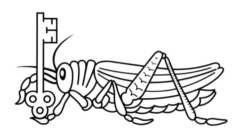

A Foreword to *Howson of Holt*

J. H. Simpson's *Howson of Holt* was first published in 1925 but is now very hard to find. This second edition reveals what a remarkable choice the Fishmongers' Company, the Governors of Gresham's School, Holt, made in 1900 for the first head of their re-founded school. George William Saul Howson created a new type of boarding school. This intimate portrait of him is a memorial of a friendship and a meditation on what makes a good school. Contemporary photographs from the school's archive bring this period to life. Simpson's unusually wide experience put him in an ideal position to describe how Howson's ideas shaped Gresham's. Both men were major contributors to the educational debate of their time about boarding and the purpose of education. At a time in the early twenty-first century when schools seem to be buried beneath ever-expanding exam programmes, league tables and statistics, this brief but revealing biography asks challenging questions about what teachers and schools should be about.

Anthony Duckworth-Chad

Past Prime Warden of the Fishmongers' Company and Chairman of the Governors of Gresham's School

Acknowledgements

The editors would like to thank John Mainstone, who first had the idea of a second edition of *Howson of Holt*. His enthusiasm and generosity in supporting the project have brought it to fruition. His son Tim Mainstone has given wise advice on all matters of design. Steve Benson's portrait of Howson in his history of Gresham's School, *I Will Plant Me a Tree*, was an invaluable source, and he has been generous in loaning books and general encouragement. Bill White, from Rendcomb College, has spent hours digging through the Rendcomb archives, and has been the most helpful of correspondents – yet another example of the ongoing relationship between Gresham's and Rendcomb. Both Headmasters, Phillip John at Gresham's and Gerry Holden at Rendcomb, have supported this edition. Chris Wood from Rendcomb and Liz Larby, the archivist at Gresham's School, helped in finding and choosing photographs as did Tony Leech. Paul Rankin made sure they appeared at their best and was responsible for the typography and layout of the book.

Introduction

The man who first showed me, among many other things, what boys could be and do if they were set free from absurd and restrictive customs was G. W. S. Howson, Headmaster of Gresham's School, Holt...

(From J. H. Simpson's, *A Schoolmaster's Harvest*, Faber and Faber, 1944)

Appointed by the Governors of Gresham's, Holt at Fishmongers' Hall in the summer of 1900 as Headmaster of their re-founded school G. W. S. Howson was a remarkable choice. Born in 1860, he came from a line of school masters and churchmen. His grandfather had been Second Master of Giggleswick and his father taught at Horton-in-Ribbersdale, Alston and Penrith. From Giggleswick School George went on to read the then new subject of Science as a Postmaster (Scholar) of Merton College, Oxford. He began his school mastering career at Newton Abbott before becoming Senior Science Master at Uppingham. As Headmaster he started afresh with staff appointments and began with only 44 pupils. 19 years later the *Times Educational Supplement* gave him the rare accolade of a full page obituary when he died in office at the age of 58, some say from sadness at the school's losses in the 1914–18 war. His vision and fresh approach to every aspect of education had earned him a prominent place in the history of 20th Century educational thinking. But when reference is made to the most significant progressive schools of that time Gresham's is seldom mentioned. Why this is so is something of a mystery.

In his Speech Day address in 1912 Howson said that a school's system of education is indicated by the character of its pupils and the reputation of its Old Boys. The range of startlingly original achievements of his school's Old Boys over the next 30 years is arguably unique and certainly vindicates what he was setting out to achieve. The list of some of them in chronological order (see the appendix for more details) cannot fail to impress: Sir John Reith, first Director General of the BBC, Ben Nicholson OM, artist, Leslie Baynes, inventor of swing wing aircraft and early pioneer of flying boats, Sir Lennox Berkeley, composer, Erskine Childers, President of Ireland, John Hayward, literary scholar, critic and friend of T. S. Eliot, Michael Spender, pioneer of aerial photographic reconnaissance, Sir Stephen Spender, writer and poet, Humphrey Spender, photographer and textile designer, Wystan Auden, poet and critic, Robert Medley, designer for the Group Theatre in London in the 1930s, Lord Simon, Solicitor General, David Keith-Lucas, developer of the jump jet, Sir Christopher Cockerell, inventor of the hovercraft, Sir Alan Hodgkin, OM, Nobel Prize winner for medicine and Master of Trinity College, Cambridge, Benjamin Britten, OM, Composer, Ian Proctor, designer of the Wayfarer Dinghy, Michael Cummings, cartoonist, Peter Brook, theatre director, Sir Martin Wood, FRS, pioneer of the MRI Scanner, David Lack, FRS, one of a number of ground breaking ornithologists from the school. Judged by the achievements of these scientists, designers and creative artists Gresham's should be included in any list of progressive schools, for creativity and originality, especially in science, were a natural product of the way the boys there were taught.

What produced this 'nest of singing birds' is much less well known than the birds themselves. The reasons for this are not easy to see. Perhaps the extreme left wing thinking of some of its old boys in the 1930's, including the spy, Donald Maclean, and the occasionally trenchant criticisms of the Honour system in the school at that time, for example by W. H. Auden in the 1930's, may have discredited it in the eyes of some. Even the willingness of the school to keep as a pupil the son of someone who became a prominent member of the IRA, Erskine Childers, was not always understood. More importantly the significant contribution Howson made to educational thinking may not have become widely known because of the school's geographical isolation. The simple fact of its not playing inter-school matches would have added to this. It did not become part of any of the natural groupings which result from them. The only exception to this was that after Howson's time Gresham's played Hockey against Gordonstoun, another remote progressive school, a fixture that introduced the Duke of Edinburgh to North Norfolk for the first time.

But, most obviously, the school itself moved away from some of the methods and thinking of Howson and his successor, J. R. Eccles, a founder member of Howson's common room who retired from the headship in 1935. There was therefore after that time not the same desire on its part to be identified as a progressive school, though some of its ethos has since always been preserved. Also, and importantly, many of the distinctive elements of Gresham's curriculum were more generally adopted so it ceased gradually to be so unusual. In Howson's address at the celebration of the 350th anniversary of the school he said, 'I hope, nay I prophesy, that our curriculum will become the model for the majority of public schools'. His prophecy turned out to be right.

The 25 years after Simpson left the common room were highly significant. Eccles kept the faith with the legacy he inherited when he was appointed Head in 1919. He preserved Howson's school. He had after all helped Howson create it. Inevitably he added his own interests and personality. Many of the school's most celebrated Old Boys were there in the 1920's and 1930's, in Eccles' time, so the influences on them came from this pair of talents and the staff they appointed.

A brief summary of the principal features of the school under both Howson and Eccles may help to put *Howson of Holt* into sharper focus. These principles can be summarised as follows. First, the curriculum: Howson, both in his application for the job and in his first prospectus, quoted the words of a highly influential educational thinker of that time, Michael Sadler, 'There is a great need in England of first class secondary schools giving a purely modern education of the highest quality based chiefly on linguistic discipline in English, French and German, going to a high point in Mathematics, teaching History, Geography and Literature searchingly and disciplining every boy in Natural Sciences – such a type of liberal education being a natural avenue to intellectual interest in modern commerce and industry.' The Governors and parents knew what they were going to get, for that was precisely what Gresham's provided. Science was at the heart of the curriculum. More than half the school, for example, were in the Natural History Society. Boys could do practicals on their own out of lesson time and the choice of subjects in the 6th form was left much to the individual. Beyond the School Certificate, on which no emphasis was placed, there were no external exams and no formal syllabus for each subject. Boys could therefore proceed through the forms at their own pace and there was no shame or loss of seniority from arriving at the 5th forms at the age of 17.

Howson also believed in the primacy of moral education inculcated by personal example, admonition and most of all in respect and trust for the boys. There was a paradox in this linking of moral education with trust. Both were uncompromisingly practised. If the impulse was firstly a moral one it also had a striking effect upon learning. An Old Boy from Eccles's time said that at the age of 16 almost half his lessons were study periods. Sir Alan Hodgkin elaborated on that: 'We were encouraged to read widely and to work on our own and this I think is the most important thing I learned at school'.

Masters taught what they wished to teach and did not necessarily

J. R. Eccles Headmaster 1919-1935

confine themselves to their own subject. The standards of scholarship were remarkable and were marked soon after Howson's appointment by awards at Oxford and Cambridge, most in science but also in History and Languages. Boys did work on their own of the highest originality, often giving talks on it to the Natural History Society: Auden, for example, lectured on Enzymes in 1924 when they were only just beginning to be understood. Music, drama and art were also taken seriously; individual precocity was encouraged and modernity respected. This must have been what attracted Benjamin Britten's parents to the school. He was allowed to go up to London from the age of 14 for music lessons.

The Honour system has been much described and frequently misunderstood. It has proved one of the most contentious of Howson's legacies. When boys first arrived at the school they had to make three promises – not to smoke, not to swear and not to commit indecency. Furthermore they promised to try to persuade any fellow pupil breaking the rules to mend his ways and in the last resort report him to his housemaster. The system was a replacement for orthodox school discipline: it did away almost completely with the schoolmaster's traditional weapons of the cane, gating and lines. Old-fashioned discipline was to be replaced by self-discipline. If that failed then the friendly persuasion of a fellow pupil was the next step. Only finally, and as a last resort, was adult authority brought to bear on the miscreant. Freedom and self-reliance were balanced by an ultimate, but seldom used, authority. This was a 'compact' or system of trust based on one of Howson's most deeply held beliefs: the innate goodness of the boys in his charge. Simpson saw it as the cornerstone on which Howson built his school. It seemed to work for, as Simpson noted, Gresham's boys were profoundly different from those of other boarding schools. 'Fresh air and Morality' were its keynotes.

But what began as a system of trust came to be seen by Auden as an instrument of fascist control. His comment that informing on others made boys 'Furtive, dishonest and unadventurous' seems to be belied by his own career and the obvious success of the school. His educational writing was confined to the social and psychological dimensions of private boarding schools for boys. He always found authority figures ridiculous, though he enjoyed regulating the lives of his friends, and when he was allowed to be, was very strict. The growth of fascism in the 1920's and 1930's loomed large in his thinking and its inexorable progress made him angry with what seemed to him like the inability of the west to deal with it. This anger pervaded his writing and thinking about education, and coloured his memories of Gresham's. However by the 1950's he was willing to admit that he had had a good education and on the whole had been very happy at school. Certainly his friends thought he was at his happiest when in the 1930's he was teaching at a liberal Quaker Prep school and his lessons were obviously inspired by many he would have had at his own school. He also retained a lifelong interest in science sparked by Gresham's – his last piece of writing on it was a letter in *Scientific American* in December 1972, less than a year before he died, on uniqueness and prematurity in scientific discovery.

Lastly, and by no means least, especially under Eccles, the school became overtly anti-establishment, encouraged free political debate and when necessary staff and pupils were willing to support unfashionable political opinions. This was what attracted many parents to send their sons there and was of course in marked contrast to most Independent Schools at that time and since. Small wonder it turned out some highly articulate and talented rebels, some of whom remained critical of their school, as they had been encouraged to be while they were there. All were encouraged to pursue personal enthusiasms and develop quickly into independent thinkers and researchers. This was the basis of the philosophy that was established by Howson and Eccles, chosen by the parents and embraced by the staff and pupils – with remarkable results. J. H. Simpson's affectionate memoir of Howson goes a long way to explaining how it all happened.

J. H. Simpson was appointed by Howson to teach at Gresham's in 1908. Like Howson, he was from a professional family of Yorkshire descent. His father had been a doctor in Rugby and Simpson attended Rugby School as both a day boy and a boarder. He studied history and classics at Pembroke College Cambridge, gaining a First in Part 1. He then took the unconventional choice of a year at the Cambridge University Day Training

College, founded by the eccentric Oscar Browning; its purpose was to train teachers in elementary schools at a time when it was often felt they needed little training. Certainly few of its trainees came from Simpson's establishment background. The choice was typical of a man who thought originally and deeply about the theory and practice of education and whose career bridged the divide between state education and public schools.

An undercurrent of Simpson's account is his dissatisfaction with conventional public boarding schools of his day. Boys were too often left to their own devices; academic standards were low and too many 'loafers' were produced by a group ethos of idle philistinism; sport, on the other hand, was worshipped. Punishment was punitive and the buildings themselves with their barred windows and locked doors seemed as grim to him as the system that sustained them. No doubt Simpson was attracted to Gresham's by its reputation as a new and different kind of school. He arrived in 1908 and became a house tutor in School House under Howson. Simpson was immediately impressed by him and they became close friends for the three years he spent at Gresham's. He taught history inspiringly well and played a lively part in the school's Debating Society where he always took a radical stance on issues of the day. In 1910 he became its President. After he left he visited Howson regularly in the holidays and joined his fishing parties to Bolton Abbey in Wharfedale which allowed pupils to see their headmaster enjoying the fly fishing he loved so much. Howson posted photos of Simpson in his fishing gear in his family album.

Howson of Holt was published in 1925, fifteen years after Simpson had left the school and six years after Howson's death, when Simpson had become the first Headmaster of Rendcomb College. It was in part an attempt to outline the uniqueness of the Headmaster and his school, reflecting his admiration and affection for Howson, as he remembered him. It is also

One of the Honours Boards in Big School

a meditation on how a Headmaster can shape a school and its pupils. For Howson of Holt read Simpson of Rendcomb. In both cases the personality and ideas of the Headmaster were paramount. Howson knew all his boys well and the closeness between him and his staff and pupils was remarkable. He invited his senior boys to wander freely into his house; they came in and out even when he had distinguished visitors such as the Master of Magdalene College, Cambridge, A. C. Benson, to dinner. He lent them his own furniture for their studies. There was, as Simpson put it, no baize door. Reciprocally, senior boys entertained their headmaster and favourite teachers to 'study teas' where they could chat together informally. Howson loved flowers and Simpson describes the amazement with which he saw a bunch of flowers on his classroom desk. It was a family atmosphere; Howson was always the patriarch and his two sisters, one of whom was known as 'Matron', provided a feminine presence for the boys.

What underpinned this sense of family was a word that Simpson often found himself using: 'kindliness'. Whatever other virtues belonged to public schools at the time, kindliness was not obviously one of them. Nor was Howson, whose physical presence and rough, burly red-faced appearance Simpson describes so clearly, an obviously tender-hearted soul – and yet this is what Simpson saw as the secret of his magnetism. Boys knew that, however forbidding Howson might seem there was a fundamental sense that he was with them and for them. When war came in 1914 they responded by writing back to their headmaster some of the most revealing public school letters from the trenches. In his *Sane Schooling* (1936) Simpson wrote: 'Three years which I had spent with that original headmaster, G. W. S. Howson, when he was at the height of his strength, had left me with a picture of a school life infinitely more happy and gracious and less ridden by convention than anything I had previously known.'

J. H.Simpson, Headmaster Rendcomb College 1920-1932

Howson himself was both an innovator and a traditionalist, following a tradition of moral education that can be traced back to Thomas Arnold at Rugby. The aim was character building. Arnold hoped to produce Christian gentlemen. Howson would not have disagreed – although his sense of religion was very different from Arnold's. His sermons were very important to him and the school; it is no accident that they are the only publicly printed record of his words. He preached only once a term; Simpson's account makes it easy to imagine the whole school hanging on to the words of the Headmaster as he preached. And yet his earnest message was always one of good conduct, not one of metaphysics or of spiritual exploration of the Christian faith.

After he left Gresham's Simpson became an Inspector of Schools for the Ministry of Education, based in Bolton, and saw a very different kind of pupil and education, as he toured elementary schools in some of the slum areas of the North West of England. There he saw poverty, and an educational system still hanging on to the Victorian payment by results scheme. He was horrified to find slates in the classroom cupboards. His career took another surprising turn when he went back to his old school, Rugby. There he managed to persuade the reformist Headmaster, Dr David, to allow him to try 'an adventure in education'. How could the typically lazy public school boy of the time, be transformed? If the same pressures that meant that a boy was reluctant to 'let the side down' in a sports team could be harnessed to the academic side, he believed the effect would be transforming: hence his experiment. He divided the thirteen-year-old boys in his Latin set into two teams who constantly competed with each other to get their answers correct. Group competition and working together was to replace individual competition. The reward for success was a collective one too – a form holiday. This kind of 'peer pressure' essentially harnessed the Honour system to an academic end.

The other, and perhaps the major, influence on Simpson was the American-born Homer Lane, a controversial figure, with ideas about educational institutions far ahead of his time. Before and during the First World War his experimental 'Little Commonwealth' in Dorset educated its 'citizens' in a way of almost untrammelled freedom and self-determination. His favourite dictum was 'You must be on the side of the child'. His clientele were junior offenders and his main aim was therapeutic: he was trying to save the boys and girls from a life of criminality. Teaching was definitely not top of his agenda. In September 1913 Homer Lane was invited to speak to the 200 boys at Gresham's School. He spoke with hands in his pockets, casually leaning forward with a slight drawl. After the talk Simpson asked diffidently if he might visit the community and see for himself. He arrived before Christmas and was so impressed by it and the charm of his host that he gave the school a motor bicycle and visited it many times afterwards. A. S. Neill, who became Headmaster of Summerhill, was Lane's keenest disciple and treated his words as nothing short of oracular. After the war he put Lane's ideas into practice and Summerhill became one the best known of progressive schools. Perhaps not surprisingly, Homer Lane was also a strong influence for a while on Wystan Auden.

For both Simpson and Howson the First World War was a watershed. 101 of Howson's boys were killed and he deeply felt the loss of what were his surrogate children. His health began to crack. Photographs show the shocking difference between the confident young headmaster and the broken man at the end of the war. By contrast Simpson enlisted into a smart regiment, studied military training and education and the way that officers and men worked together in harmony. He came out of the war relatively unscathed, ready to face new challenges and to implement what he had learned from his experience of education which ranged from traditional public schools, to a 'progressive' boarding school and to elementary schools in the North.

He had just applied for the post of Professor of Education at Leeds when he was approached with a fascinating proposal.

The rich philanthropist Noel Wills (who was later to write a biography of Homer Lane) wanted to establish a school for working class children which would prepare them for entry into public schools – a kind of precursor of the Direct Grant System. Boys from elementary schools would be funded by Gloucester County Council to attend a boarding school. Simpson, like Howson in 1900, was presented with a more or less blank slate to write on. It was – to use his own title – an adventure in education, an opportunity to give working class boys the

Rendcomb College

chance to experience what had hitherto been available only to the more comfortably off, to transfer the boarding school from the hands of the rich middle and upper classes to the working class. He immediately insisted on two most significant changes. He wanted his school to prepare boys for work or university and certainly not for public schools. Secondly, he added some fee-payers to create a social mix. Rendcomb became a kind of laboratory to see how the ideas he had absorbed would work in practice.

Howson had begun his school in 1900 with 7 boarders: Simpson 11. Initially at Rendcomb there were only four members of staff. Simpson had first met Charles Osborne as a keen sixth form debater at Gresham's; Osborne then read History at Oxford before returning to his old school to teach. Simpson immediately recruited him to Rendcomb, together with his wife who had taught French at Gresham's 'by the direct method'. They were to form the nucleus of his staff. Along with them was the young son of Homer Lane, who was doing a 'gap year' before going up to Balliol College, Oxford. Simpson followed Howson's example and built the school around his own personality and family. Pupils of both headmasters spoke of them in remarkably similar terms as charismatic leaders, as examples and as friends.

Both Gresham's and Rendcomb were set in beautiful isolated countryside. Free time and freedom were of great importance and the boys of Rendcomb were allowed to roam the Gloucestershire countryside after Sunday Chapel just as Gresham's boys could bike round the North Norfolk Coast. Simpson had noted how important house plays were at Gresham's for bringing the boys a sense of common purpose. He set about building an outdoor theatre on the lines of the Woodland Theatre at Gresham's. Fagging was light at Gresham's, but banned at Rendcomb. Simpson, like Howson, rejected the pervasive cult of the sportsman. All the apparatus of colours for games – blazers, even scrum caps – were banned. The worship of games was replaced not by Swedish Drill, but by something very like it – PE. Formal orders, marks and outside examinations were at a very minimal level. Masters were told that they could give marks – so long as they did not add them up! Simpson's aim was, like Howson's, to avoid producing the typical public school product that both looked down on as superior and falsely conventional.

The word Simpson chose to end his account of Rendcomb with (which he called 'Churnside') was 'individuality'.

Simpson's views on education had become more radical than Howson's. They were based, as were many of his postwar generation, on the iniquities of the class system and the divisions in society it both mirrored and perpetuated – The Eloi and the Morlocks of H. G. Wells's *The Time Machine*.

Howson and his sisters and the first seven borders
(Miss Rosa Howson on the left, Mary Standing)

Simpson felt the public school system – even under its best exponents such as Howson – was doomed because it did not address the problems of social equality. In Gloucestershire Simpson gained a reputation as 'a Bolshevik' – carrying on Howson's own reputation of the Headmaster as a dangerous radical in Norfolk. He aimed to break down the rigidity of class distinctions in his school and paid great attention to the social mix Rendcomb had. When a boy arrived he was given a school uniform and a Sunday suit so that clothes could not mark out distinctions of rich and poor. He was delighted that, whatever differences existed to start with, soon the boys mixed on equal terms. One boy, he was pleased to report, spent his holidays with two of his friends. One was in a country house; the other in the cottage of an out of work miner. Howson himself had no such social awareness. Simpson noted his lack of interest in the sons of the tradesmen of Holt who came as his day boys.

The second major difference was the importance Simpson and other progressive Headmasters, such as A. S. Neill, ascribed to the General Meeting. He followed Homer Lane's practice and set up a weekly meeting. Today's 'school councils' are watered-down versions of the powerful role Simpson gave to his assembly. Members of staff were not allowed to attend. Simpson sat quietly writing notes, occasionally adding a comment or question, as this democratic body of pupils decided school policy. The Games Committee decided what sports should be played and organized pitches and fixtures, the Shopkeeper ran the school shop, and the Committee even elected a 'banker' to tax boys on their weekly pocket money in order to provide school facilities.

After leaving Rendcomb in 1932, Simpson became Principal of the College of St Mark and St John in Chelsea, a Church of England training college, and Chairman of Governors of several London schools. He helped to prepare the Spens report in the late 1930s and advised the government on educational issues. He continued to be ahead of his time, supporting co-education, sex education, mixed ability learning and a kind of school that came to be known as comprehensive. At Rendcomb, his successor was Dennis Lee-Browne who had been at Gresham's when Howson's influence was still pervasive. Hence Howson's ideas were filtered through to another generation and the remarkable link between the two schools persisted. (It continues to this day. The Headmaster of Gresham's Prep School at present is the son of Anthony Quick who was Headmaster of Rendcomb for many years.)

Unlike Simpson, Howson left no written theory; no diaries; no account of how to build a school. He was an intuitive rather than a systematic thinker – 'an artist in school life', as Simpson called him. Simpson's memoir aimed to put this right and give Howson the place he deserved in the story of the development of education in England. He chose his title carefully. It suggested a line of great Headmasters: Arnold of Rugby, Thring of Uppingham, Sanderson of Oundle. Howson of Holt could stand worthily beside them as one whose influence spread far beyond their own schools and the public school system they worked in. When Simpson died in March 1959 his obituary in *The Times* began by describing him as 'a forward-looking man who during the first three decades of the present century led the way in transforming school curricula and methods, and, more importantly, improving greatly relations between pupils and teachers'. That was Howson's legacy.

Hugh Wright and John Smart

HOWSON OF HOLT

First published in 1925

PREFACE

THIS little volume is in no sense a history of Gresham's School since its re-birth in 1900, nor is it an "authorized" life of G. W. S. Howson. I have written it for the most part from my own memories, modified, of course, by the conversation and letters of friends. In so far as it contains opinions as well as facts, I do not claim that they are the opinions of anyone but myself.

My object in writing is not solely, or even primarily, to attempt to describe a remarkable man, in whose personality many of his pupils and colleagues found a force which will influence them to the end of their lives. I believe that many who have no personal reason for being interested in Gresham's School, will appreciate the educational importance of what Howson accomplished. He did not court publicity while he lived; and although in the last six years the public have become increasingly familiar with the name of Gresham's School, comparatively few people yet realize how interesting were the ideas which this fearless and original head master found there an opportunity of putting into practice.

The greater number of my memories naturally come from the years 1908-1910, when I knew the school from inside. Howson was, I believe, at that time at the height of his creative power. Whenever in these pages I try to describe the school, I am thinking of the school as it was in those years. My understanding, however, of much that I saw in that short and happy period was only made possible by the many talks I had with Howson in later years. Fortunately for myself, I was able to visit Holt frequently between 1911 and 1915, and to join several of Howson's holiday parties of boys and old boys.

I do not know whether I have written more about the school or about its head master, and I have made no attempt to keep the two separate. If this is a fault in arrangement, it seems to me to be inevitable to the subject. The man and his work cannot be separated, for in his work the man expressed himself with extraordinary completeness. Howson does not easily fit into the ordinary conception of a great head master. He was not one of the old Olympians, under whom so many of my generation were brought up; remote, mysterious, they made us chiefly aware of their presence when they launched their thunderbolts from the chapel pulpit. Nor was he a great teacher, who influenced his school primarily through the intellectual appeal which he made to his sixth form. He did not belong to the modern organizers, who are so interested in the curriculum, and he was no scientific schoolmaster, who related his work either to current theory, or to a national system of education. I think of Howson as first of all an *artist in school life*. He took the common metal which comes into the schoolmaster's hand and fashioned out of it by the unsparing use of personal influence a community in many respects surprisingly different from other schools. Quite early in his career as a head master, or before it began, he had a clear vision of how a school ought, as he believed, to live. Before many years passed, he began to give form to that vision; and at last the school life which he desired-expressing his ideals, hopes, tastes, prejudices-came into being.

J.H.S.

Rendcomb, 1925.

HOWSON OF HOLT

IR JOHN GRESHAM'S Free Grammar School at Holt, to which Howson was appointed as head master in the year 1900, was at that time practically unknown outside the County of Norfolk. A foundation of the Elizabethan age, its affairs had been entrusted to the Fishmongers' Company, and it had served local educational needs for several centuries with credit, and sometimes even with distinction, sending a number of boys to Cambridge University. Its fortunes seem rather to have declined, and towards the end of last century its position was insignificant. We used to hear from local residents amusing stories about the sleepy and unambitious days, before the renaissance of 1900. There is no reason, however, to think that the school was much more inefficient than a number of similar small local schools, before the legislation of 1902 rejuvenated them, or altered them out of recognition.

A great change, however, was at hand. Shortly before the end of the century, a number of leases of land belonging to the Trust fell in, and the property would henceforth bring in a considerably larger rental. The Governing Body, faced with the prospect of a largely increased income, decided virtually to restart the school, to spend a large sum of money on the erection of modern buildings, and to engage a new head master and staff. It was a great opportunity for the right man; still, the fact remains that the school, when Howson went to it, was a small country grammar school with no very impressive tradition and no prominence in the world of education. The bare facts of the school's growth under Howson are striking. He started with forty-four boys (seven of them boarders) and a staff of four masters. The new School House, and the block of buildings containing the Big School and classrooms, were formally opened in October 1903. By 1903 the number of boys had reached one hundred, and at the time of his death in

5

1919 it stood at two hundred and forty: of these two hundred and twenty were boarders. If accommodation had permitted, as Howson himself had wished, the number could have been far greater, for Gresham's School was by this time well known throughout the country. It was entitled, in fact, to take rank among the recognized public schools.

It would be a very misleading summary, however, of Howson's work to say that he had added another name to the list of public

Gresham's School

schools. Those who knew Gresham's School intimately, when he was at the height of his power, are aware that his greatness lay not in creating a school true to a recognized type, but in creating a school in many respects unique. Gresham's School advanced so rapidly because it stood for something new and different. Just for that reason it is natural to wonder how far Howson's educational ideals were the direct result of his personal experience, and what lessons the other schools which

6

he had known had taught him, either as warning or example.

. . . .

Howson's father had been the head master of a school in the North of England. His family connection with the teaching profession did not, perhaps, count for much in his career; but in a certain bluntness of speech, and practical shrewdness, as well as in the peculiar type of his humour, he always belonged to the North rather than to the South. If he did not like North Country people best, I think he understood them best. There is a kind of culture, represented principally by the public schools and older universities. It is associated, perhaps wrongly, rather with the South and West of England than with the North. It shows itself not least in a reverence for the past, and a regard for the form as well as for the spirit. Of this way of looking at life, Howson was always inclined to be impatient. After spending several years at Giggleswick, where his grandfather had been at one time second master, Howson proceeded to Oxford in 1879, as a science scholar of Merton College. He seldom spoke in my hearing of his undergraduate days, but I gained the impression that he had no great opinion of the Merton of his time, or of the Oxford tutorial system as he knew it. Speaking at an Old Greshamian dinner at Oxford in 1912, he said, no doubt with admirable sense, but with something less than conventional loyalty to his old college, that if he could have had his time at Oxford over again, he would have chosen to be a Demy of Magdalen. I do not know whether there dated from this time his later rather contemptuous attitude to dons in general, whom he regarded as too much inclined to allow their pupils to drift in their own way, without advice or reproof. Academically his Oxford career was successful, for in 1883 he obtained a First Class in the Final Honours School of Natural Science. Those who knew Howson only in later life find it difficult to think of him as a man of science, for he did no science teaching at

Gresham's, and he was obviously much less interested in facts and abstract theory than in human beings. It would be safe, I think, to assume that it was his interest in boys, rather than any particular enthusiasm for his subject, that made him want to he a schoolmaster.

His first teaching post was at Newton Abbott, then a school of considerable repute. Here he seems to have been happy in his work and friendships, and he conceived a love for the moors and streams of Devon which he never lost. There were times when he thought of Devon as a place to which he might retire when he had finished his work. Of the school itself he used to speak with regard and interest, but I never heard him express any admiration for its educational merits, or give any sign that his stay there had deeply influenced him.

He was far more deeply, and perhaps decisively, influenced by his fourteen years at Uppingham, where he was appointed as science master in 1886. They were all important years for Howson's development as a schoolmaster, for in them he had his only direct experience of the large public school. It is, I think, true, and I hope it may be said without offence, that Howson never saw the public-school system quite at its best. He went to Uppingham attracted by the great name of Thring; but Thring's regime ended two years later, and the years which followed his death would probably be regarded by most Uppinghamians as not the most distinguished period in the history of their distinguished school. Nor was Howson's position one to enable him to appreciate what was best in the school. He was in a minority-an Oxford man among colleagues of whom the most influential were mainly Cambridge, a science master when science was still the Cinderella of public-school subjects, a non-athletic master in a school where athletics counted for much. In a public school, where the boundary line between masters and boys is sharply defined, and games are the

Howson the young schoolmaster at Newton Abbott

predominant interest, the master who is genuinely interested, as Howson was, in the out-of school life of the boys, but does not take part in the recognized school games, must not be surprised if he is regarded by the boys as a busybody. An interest in boys and an affection for them, which cannot be expressed along the few conventional channels, are regarded with suspicion. A desire for intimacy and friendship is stupidly mistaken for a

9

wish to interfere, and to make discoveries. Such a reputation, though it is founded on no real basis, and is at first regarded only half seriously, will persist and grow until it becomes a kind of school legend. Finally it is accepted by older people, who ought to know better. Probably it would be a fair summary of Howson's position at Uppingham to say that with one (probably rather stupid) section he was definitely unpopular; that there were always some among masters and boys who appreciated his remarkable qualities, and knew that what he stood for was essentially fine, though it might not appeal to the Uppingham orthodoxy of the moment; but that the majority regarded him rather indifferently, as a master having no great influence in the councils of the school. The last fact must always come as a surprise to those who knew him only at Holt – that he does not seem to have been one of the men who counted; and it shows how quick and vigorous was his growth when he could work in conditions of his own making. One, who was a prominent boy at Uppingham at the end of Howson's time there, has told me how he was struck by the contrast which he found, when he visited Howson at Holt soon after taking his degree. He went there rather inclined, perhaps, to patronize the head of an obscure grammar school. He remembered him merely as a not very important member of the Uppingham staff. And he found a man who was not only very much the master of his own house, but was full of confidence in the bigness of his work, and his ability to make other people recognize it.

. . . .

I do not wish to imply that Howson learned nothing at Uppingham, or that he was a rebel against everything that he found there. In one respect he was entirely true to public school orthodoxy, in his belief that the schoolmaster's first duty is to train character (whatever we may mean by that useful phrase), rather than to stir the intellect. Certain other characteristics of his were also well within the tradition; for example his rather contemptuous attitude to educational theory and theorists, and, I will add, though others will disagree, his rather Erastian view of the place of religion in school life. It is quite certain however, that when he first went to Holt, and for a number of years afterwards, Howson thought of the school that he was creating as quite definitely a departure from the ordinary public schools, and outside their number. In his later years, and particularly, perhaps, after the outbreak of the war, his attitude in this matter

Howson's Study at Uppingham

underwent a change. He liked to think of Gresham's playing in the national crisis a part comparable, relatively to its size, with that played by the historic foundations. He felt a justifiable pride in the position among the well-known boarding schools to which Gresham's had been raised by his notable efforts. There were some who viewed this change with disfavour, and thought that Howson lost some of his power and independence after, as one old boy wrote to me, "he coquetted with the idea

11

of Holt as a Public School" Be that as it may, in earlier years he often spoke of the public schools with disparagement; and he made no secret that their standards were not, if he could help it, to be the standards of Gresham's.

It is important for an understanding of Howson's work to notice what points in the public-school system he particularly disliked, for they were not, in all cases, those most vigorously attacked by other reformers. He hated some of the recognized abuses as much as anyone. The narrowness of the curriculum of thirty years ago, and the then privileged position of the classics, made him indignant. So did rigid systems of superannuation, and any tendency to judge boys too much by intellect alone; he always had a more observant eye for intellectual than for moral priggishness. He was, too, the bitter foe of athleticism. But what he really disliked most about the public schools was their own particular kind of freedom – freedom, as he saw it, for a boy to drift the wrong way, with nobody in particular to restrain him. That was the point in which he most unsparingly criticized most housemasters: that they left their boys too much alone, and did not, as he would say, help them to fight their battles. He had a vivid, and indeed exaggerated, conception both of the barrier between boys and masters at public schools, and of the barrier between the life of home and school – real as those evils are. For the schoolboy conventions, shielded by those barriers and in turn reinforcing them, he had no sympathy whatever; to him they were purely mischievous or frivolous. I am not sure that the last word does not convey most accurately his conception of the normal public-school pleasant but aimless frivolity, in which a boy could drift for four or five years, with only a random chance of learning that life had a more serious aspect.

Howson cherished, as long as he lived, the belief that school life could be better, happier, and more beautiful than it is usually found to be; that a boy was capable of obeying a higher code (higher, that is to say, as judged by ethical standards) than the conventions of schoolboys commonly allow; and that it was above everything else his duty as a schoolmaster so to mould the characters of his boys, that his ideals should determine the character and life of the school which he hoped to create. It is easy enough to recall, but less easy to describe, the picture of Holt life that I took away with me at the end of my first term

Dining room, School House

in 1908, eight years after Howson started his work. If I attempt to reproduce the vivid impressions made upon my mind, it is because I believe that they would have been shared by most young masters going there, as I did, with many of the ordinary public-school beliefs and prejudices. I know, too, from what they have told me, that similar impressions (with certain obvious differences) were gained by boys who were transferred to Gresham's from other schools.

13

"Sunshine and Puritanism" was how a friend of mine described his first impressions. So summary a description is bound to be misleading, but he would have been nearer the mark with "Fresh Air and Morality." Certainly there was a wonderful sense of freshness and cleanliness about the school, arising not solely from the fact that it was exposed to some of the healthiest air in England. The buildings had their faults aesthetically, and their very newness seemed raw to some people, but they were light, and airy, and convenient, and they were cleaner and more cheerful than any school buildings I had ever known. There were no dusty passages, dark corners, narrow windows, and iron bars; and out beyond the playing-fields and their woodland fringe the Sunday walker could tramp across wind-swept heaths, till he came within sight of the sea.

A freshness, too, of mind and spirit, seemed to animate both the older and the younger members of this attractive community. To a newcomer to the staff, this showed itself first, perhaps, in his colleagues. He found in them a belief in and enthusiasm for their work, altogether different from the cynicism and boredom that make many common-rooms so depressing. He was quickly made welcome, and as almost every one of his colleagues seemed interested in many sides of the school life, he usually slipped naturally into taking a useful and happy part in all kinds of school activities, though in some of them, perhaps, he had not previously been interested. Soon after Howson's death, one speaking with the fullest knowledge, wrote of "the spirit of brotherhood," that he created in his school. It was not long before anyone working at all sympathetically with Howson realized something of this "brotherhood." We were not paragons of virtue, but very ordinary schoolmasters, with human differences of opinion and quite human ways of expressing them. Only, in our dealings with each other we were saved, I think, from some of that pettiness, which is one of the curses of our profession, by the sense that we were engaged

14

together in a remarkable enterprise. There was a feeling, most refreshing in itself, that the actions of our common life were not settled by convention or some half-understood tradition, but were rather parts of a consistent scheme of life, planned by a man working for an object, and every one of us could in some degree understand what that object was.

What impressions of the boys did a newcomer get during his first few days? To a new master they appeared remarkably happy, unexpectedly friendly, well-mannered (sometimes too consciously polite), ready to learn, widely interested, and ingenuous. To a boy from another school, as I have been assured, they appeared unusually friendly, strangely almost uncomfortably – quiet and well behaved, amazingly free from even the mildest swearing and indecency in their language, keen on work and fair in their methods, conscious, it seemed, that they were expected by authority to lead a certain kind of life, and surprisingly anxious for that reason to do so. "People here," remarked a boy whose experience of a public school had been unhappy, "seem to do things not because they are made to, but because they think they are right." So far as it went, his remark could hardly have been put better.

As time passed, these first impressions were confirmed, and underlying causes became apparent. An observant master realized that the friendliness was not, as he may have thought, merely the rather exaggerated welcome of a newcomer; nor were the happiness and willingness to learn accidental. These qualities sprang from three facts, which were the basis of the life of the school – the boys were free from the tyrannical conventions prevailing in most public schools; they were trusted; and owing to Howson's Honour System, to be explained later, they were on terms of confidence with their house-masters.

These three facts, working together and interconnected, caused the freshness and spontaneity, so pleasantly surprising to anyone straight from an ordinary public school. He realized almost at once that the artificial barrier (for there is also a natural barrier of age) between masters and boys had been to a great extent demolished. The boys met older people without suspicion, and without shyness; they were not for a moment on the defensive. When I saw something of the life of the boarding houses, I realized how much less separate than usual were the "boys' side" and the "private side." The traditional green baize door had disappeared. Howson would have dismissed a good deal of modern cant about a school being "only another home" with one of his contemptuous grunts; but in his own house he laboured successfully, with the devoted help of his two sisters, to make his boys feel that they belonged to a domestic circle, and to let them enjoy some of the kindly and gracious influences, of which boys at school are too often deprived. He was a keen collector of old furniture, and china, and glass; and it is typical of him that these beautiful things were not kept only in his own rooms, but overflowed into the passages and the dining-hall (a really noble room) and, in the case of the furniture, even into the boys' studies. And flowers, when they were procurable, were everywhere. He knew their refining influence. I suppose that it only proves the narrowness of my own previous training, that it was almost a shock, when for the first time I had to teach in his classroom, and was confronted with a vase of flowers on his desk.

In another way, too, Howson was extraordinarily successful in drawing school and home life together. He had a wonderful way of making parents staying at Holt, and other guests as well, feel that they belonged to the place. He was essentially a host by temperament, as well as by policy and necessity, and his gift in this direction helped him considerably in building up the school. There were deeper reasons, however, why masters

A sixth form study

and boys at Holt were on such agreeable terms. Usually they are estranged for two reasons – first, because in so many of the most important questions of life it is traditional for masters to preserve an attitude of silence, or of obvious insincerity; secondly, because both sides know (though they may pretend the contrary) that, when they are away from their masters, the boys think, speak, and act according to an altogether different standard. Now it would be true to say of Holt – and this is what

17

the new boy from another school might find so perplexing – that to a quite remarkable extent boys adopted and carried out, when they were by themselves, the standards set before them by authority. If masters and boys were not artificially separated, neither were boys of different ages. Close friendships between older and younger boys were not encouraged. Howson definitely disliked them; but he would have disliked still more, I think, a rigid caste system, which allowed boys in the same house to remain total strangers. It was just as natural at Gresham's,

The first First XV (1900)

as it would have been unnatural at some other schools, for a sixth-form boy and a new boy, if they happened to leave their boarding-house at the same time, to walk to school together engaged in friendly conversation. I have chosen a trivial incident for an example; but I have known it to strike a new master with considerable surprise.

Not least did the prevailing spontaneity and *camaraderie* show themselves in the regular school games. Games rightly take an important place in school life, and at first sight they were much the same at Gresham's as elsewhere. They were played nearly as keenly, though not perhaps with any extraordinary skill. But the spirit was different, and it may be expressed by saying that games were regarded sanely, and not devotionally.

As a result, I am sure that the younger boys, at any rate, enjoyed their games more than they do at schools which maintain a cult

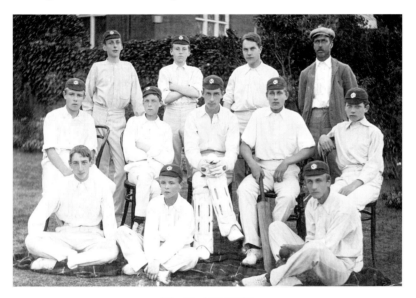

The First XI (1900)

of "solemn athleticism." It was a gain, too, that both masters and older boys who were not particularly good at games, judged by the standard of public school elevens and fifteens, could play with enjoyment, and without feeling that they were in any way absurd. I have most grateful memories of the second game of cricket, a refuge of the older boys who were not gifted at the game (a kind of disillusioned intelligentsia) where one could spend a most enjoyable afternoon, playing gloriously bad cricket in decidedly humorous surroundings, without feeling that one was committing any kind of sacrilege. I think, too that the sociability of the games, serious and half-serious alike, was increased by the fact that they were mainly organized on a school rather than a house basis, though there was also the usual system of house matches.

It was partly because games did not claim too much attention, though there were other causes too, that other out-of-school interests were able to thrive so well. I am thinking not so much of organized societies, though they also flourished, as of private hobbies and lines of study. What always struck me was that at Holt a boy who showed any real skill or enthusiasm, in however strange a direction, was not regarded as an undesirable "freak," though he might arouse some good-humoured amusement, but as a valued possession. His house could be proud of him. Of the organized activities the one counting for most was acting. Howson believed wholeheartedly in the value of acting for boys, provided that he could be satisfied (not always an easy matter) that the plays to be acted were, to use a favourite word of his, ethically "helpful." Every summer a play of Shakespeare was produced out of doors in the theatre. This had been hollowed out of the hillside in the school wood. These school plays were admirable, not so much for the acting, though that was creditable, as for the general spirit of hard and cheerful work in which they were undertaken, and for the skilful use of the musical resources of the school. More spontaneous, and for that reason, perhaps, more educative, were the house plays given in the winter terms. These sometimes reached a surprisingly high standard.

Perhaps it was because there were so many things to interest boys, but I am inclined to think it was still more on account of the almost filial relation in which they often stood to their house masters, that there was no loafing element in the school.

A solemn moment from As You Like It *in the Woodland Theatre*

Of course, there were a few cheerfully idle people, though they did not boast about it. But there was not that depressing type of boy found in many large schools (usually about the fourth or

21

fifth forms) who, unless he happens to excel in games, is merely bored and indifferent. He has no academic ambitions, is not particularly interested in anything, and nobody is particularly interested in him. His housemaster does not think of him as "useful to the house," and he has not the ability to win any form of distinction. I cannot remember any group of boys at Holt corresponding to that description. The whole atmosphere of the place made such an attitude impossible, and in particular a boy was saved from one kind of discouragement by knowing that with at least one older person he was on terms of genuine confidence.

It was, I think, because mental loafing was almost impossible, that the physical loafer was not apparent. Although there is no reason to think that the standard of physique was above the average (in fact it was very likely rather below the average, for Holt's reputation for healthiness naturally brought it more than its share of delicate boys), Gresham boys struck visitors as rather unusually brisk and alert. There were those who attributed the absence of slouching wholly to the ban upon trouser pockets; but I am inclined to think that there were psychological causes more influential.

To the assistant master at Gresham's the freedom from schoolboy conventions was apparent most of all in the attitude of the boys to their work. They were extraordinarily easy to teach, because they were anxious to learn, and it seemed to be the natural thing to work hard. If I say briefly that it was regarded as good form to work hard, and bad form, or at any rate rather silly, to be idle, it will not, perhaps, sound very impressive to anyone who has not taught in a public school. To anyone who has had that experience it will mean a good deal. There was no vestige of an idea that to be idle was the sign of a "good fellow," or that there was anything in the least contemptible in being interested in one's work, or in talking about it out of school. I often used to hear at meals discussions that would not have been out of place in the class-room, both when I was lunching in one of the house dining-halls, and at those delightful "study teas," where, by an admirable arrangement, it was possible for the older boys to return the hospitality they had received from masters.

The readiness to be interested, and to work cheerfully when the lessons, as must inevitably happen sometimes, could not be made interesting, together with the absence of unfair work, made one's teaching delightful. I can remember classes where the problem was not how to make the boys do enough work, but how to prevent the more enthusiastic ones from doing too much work out of school.

Howson did not discard the use of "marks," but they were not emphasized (there was no need for them to be), and the absence of so much of the usual machinery made one feel that inside the class-room, as well as outside, one was engaged upon the essentials: that first things came first.

Form discipline, too, unless a man was preternaturally "raggable," was an easy matter. I have sometimes wondered whether a mastership at Holt was not almost too easy an apprenticeship for a man who was going on to teach elsewhere. A young master thoroughly enjoying himself, but faced by the financial problem which the small salaries at that time presented, might think of the problem not so much as "Am I being paid enough for the work I am doing?" as "Is this delightful existence a luxury that I can afford?"

I have said that the boys were trusted, though I shall have to explain later in what sense I use the word. At any rate, one of the refreshing features of the school life was the absence of signs that it was expected that the boys would do wrong, when they were left to themselves. There were none of those obvious precautions, only inciting to the crime that they are designed to prevent. No barred windows, locked doors, or places put, for no reasons understood by the boys, "out of bounds." It was part of Howson's policy, too, to have no printed rules. This did not mean, of course, that there were not a great many things which boys knew perfectly well that they had to refrain from doing. Quite the contrary. In some respects Holt was emphatically a community living according to rule, with its own notions of what was right and wrong. But Howson preferred other means than the printed rulebook to make boys live up to his standards.

One might take, as an example of this, the system of roll-call, used on half-holidays or before chapel on Sunday. The cynic, or indeed the ordinary observer, might notice that it was a system depending entirely upon the honesty of the boys; any two boys in collusion could make it ridiculous. Yet it was extraordinarily seldom abused. Another example is the manner of spending Sunday. At most boarding schools the organization of Sunday is determined by an uneasy compromise between three conflicting feelings; the natural disinclination of the masters to teach or supervise on Sunday more than they can help, their fear of public opinion if they allow ordinary school games and occupations, and their even greater fear that, if the boys are left too long to their own devices, they will "get into mischief." Howson made no attempt to fill up Sunday, and in consequence both masters and boys benefited from a recreative and happy day. There were no Sunday scripture lessons. Chapel services were short. There were long afternoons of freedom. No doubt Sunday afternoon was not always spent wisely, but I believe that everyone who knew the life of the school from inside would agree that the freedom of Sunday brought great happiness and remarkably little "mischief."

Quite soon, probably before he had seen much of the actual life of the boys, the young master would realize that one characteristic of the school was the comparative absence of punishments. There were no "lines," a minimum of impositions, and very little "keeping in." Corporal punishment was extremely rare, and when it took place was sometimes, as a boy who had known sterner measures remarked, "of a rather lady-like character. If boys at all "did things because they were made to" they were not "made to" by the usual appeal to fear, or at any rate to fear as expressed in the traditional apparatus of prohibitions and penalties. And before long the idea of punishments of the old kind seemed almost ridiculous, seeing how sensitive were the boys to rebuke or encouragement, and how scrupulously conscientious they were, not only those in positions of special trust, to do what they thought was demanded of them.

I can recall instances of this conscientiousness which were at first almost alarming. I remember how a prefect, who was doing special work with me in my room, refused a cup of tea in the middle of discussing "Mill's Liberty" because his housemaster would not approve of tea in school hours. Or how another boy ran post-haste to his house to begin a period of private study (though he had a good reason for being late, having been detained by a master) because he was "expected to start work when the clock struck the hour."

These are small instances, but similar actions were continually striking the eye, till it was borne in upon the observer that here was a community permeated, through and through, with a desire for what it conceived to be right conduct. The end of every activity, one was reminded, was, in an adult and not always very wide sense of the word, a *moral* one.

It must be admitted, for I want to be honest, that some of these reminders were at times rather tiresome. Both older boys, who were beginning to think for themselves, and young masters, whose under graduate days were not far behind, found it not

25

always possible to breathe the rarified moral atmosphere without allowing them selves an occasional smile; but the smile did not necessarily imply any disloyalty to the ideals of the school. I confess that I felt sorry for a colleague who, having been invited to coach a house play, and having spent many hours in rehearsing and producing a perfectly innocuous farce, was informed that his production was "neither helpful nor humorous." I understood, too, the rather cynical remark of an experienced observer of schools, who once said to me "Gresham's? Yes, a fine school, a very fine school. But isn't there altogether too much moral tone about it?" Some of us, I think, felt that the idealism of the place would not have suffered from a more lively criticism, and a keener sense of humour. In a small and secluded community mutual admiration is terribly easy. But, after all, it did one no great harm to refrain from using the word "damn" for three months on end, or in the holidays to be chaffingly accused by one's friends of becoming a prig. Fortunately it was possible to be sometimes youthfully flippant and restive about trifles, and yet to retain a deep affection for the school and the man who inspired it.

. . . .

However unsuccessful I may have been in trying to describe the life of Gresham's, I believe I have made it clear that the boys did, for some reason or other, live a kind of life different from that of other schools. There remains the problem – how was this actually brought about?

From the beginning Howson was confident that Gresham's would grow to be something much more than a merely local school, however admirable. At the end of his first term, speaking to his handful of boys in the hall of the Old School House, he told them that the greatness of their privilege lay in the "fact that you are laying the foundations of the traditions of what

One of Howson's first boarders: Reginald Preston, b. 1891

many of us hope will one day be a great school. . . . It is our wish, and it should be yours, that you shall be proud to say 'I, too, was at Gresham's School.'"

Before I say anything more about him as man and schoolmaster, it will be advisable to consider what causes, other than his own personality and methods, contributed to his success. It is no disparagement of a man who took this opportunity so ably as Howson, to say that the opportunity was a good one.

Nobody who has ever visited Holt will deny that he was fortunate in his *place*, and it is equally true that he was fortunate in his *time*. Criticism of the public schools at the beginning of the century was becoming articulate and constructive. Howson did not appeal, and did not want to appeal, to cranks. "This is not the kind of school," he said the second time I met him, "where, if a boy is not good at arithmetic, he is allowed to keep rabbits instead." But he did appeal to the growing public among the professional and business classes that wanted some sane

The Old School House (1900)

alternative to the old regime. In particular, he was ready to meet the cry of the day for "more science." The knowledge that he was providing what many parents throughout the country were anxiously seeking, constantly encouraged Howson in his work. Moreover, parents who have deliberately taken the step of sending their sons to a new and practically unknown school, are perhaps more ready than others to support the head master's policy. Certainly Holt in early days, as Howson would have been the first to agree, was fortunate in its parents.

Compared with many head masters, too, he must be accounted fortunate in his Governors. We used to wonder, as we listened to the rather ponderous rhetoric of Speech Day, how many of the Governors had the slightest idea for how remarkable a school they were responsible. Some few of them, however, certainly appreciated the man and his work; and as a body they were evidently proud of the material growth of the school, and practised the great negative virtue of non-interference.

I have heard it said that Howson was fortunate in his staff. I would agree, with the reservation that much of what might seem to be due to good fortune, was due to his skill in selecting masters, and his power of helping them. More than this, however, must be said of the invaluable help which he received throughout his years at Holt from his second master, who succeeded at his death to the head mastership. It was not only that Howson had always in his second master a colleague who accepted his standards, and shared his moral enthusiasm. In the pioneer days, when new ideas had to be originated and woven into the fabric of school life, it must have made all the difference to the head master that he had someone of untiring energy and great driving force, to help to apply his principles in detail. The second master touched school life at many points. In some of these Howson was only secondarily interested. He was known to be in absolute sympathy with the head master's ideals; and his personal example of enthusiasm and thoroughness in so many activities was one of the strongest creative forces of the school. To his younger colleagues he gave an example of loyalty, industry, and single-minded devotion to the school, making both for encouragement and unity.

Finally, it ought to be remembered that Howson had one important material advantage for building his school. The education provided at Gresham's was remarkably inexpensive. Even before the war there were few schools, if any, offering conditions at all resembling those of Gresham's for about seventy pounds a year.

. . . .

When all is said, however, it was Howson himself who made Gresham's School. He was the architect, and the chief builder. The spectacle of any man of his strength working towards a clearly conceived end would have been inspiring; but his particular character, ideals, and methods determined the unique qualities of the school. His character and his work must be considered together. Consciously and unconsciously he centred the work round himself; for his ideal of school government was a kindly autocracy, working through personal influence, and his personality was essentially one to lead or to dominate. He was not fitted by temperament to be *primus inter pares*.

People who had heard of Howson as the successful schoolmaster were usually surprised by their first impressions, when they met him. There was nothing traditionally academic in his appearance and manner. The heavy, almost clumsy, body, florid complexion, and rather abrupt way of speaking suggested the successful man of affairs, rather than the man of books and ideas; and the suggestion was in a sense true. Howson's mind was not narrowly scholastic, but one that might have made him prominent in many walks of life other than the one he had chosen. He had a quiet decision of manner and a keen glance betokening at once a man of unusual power and discernment. Still, Howson was not one of whom it might be said especially that he carried his character in his face. As he would come walking down the top corridor from his classroom, with his rather rolling gait, his face flushed with the exertion of teaching, and his mortar board slightly atilt, he presented a formidable, and almost truculent, appearance, quite at variance with his real sympathy and delicacy of feeling. Far more expressive of his nature was the welcome –unforgettable to many of us – given to the old pupil or colleague, when he entered the study door after a long absence – the genial grunt as he jerked himself out of his deep chair, the keen and kindly scrutiny with head bent back, as he peered through or over his glasses, grasping one's hand, the spontaneous and invariably appropriate word of greeting, that gave one at once the feeling of being received again into the fold.

It was not everyone who liked Howson at once, or realized his bigness of heart and sincerity. I have known people, both boys and adults, who never felt comfortable in his presence. He gave them the impression that he was applying the intellectual probe, in order to pass a moral judgment. They felt somehow that they were being "got at," an impression some times strengthened by his rather one-sided form of humour. There were others who, without trying to understand the apparent contradictions of his nature – the strange combination of shrewd and subtle mind, strong impulses, and tenacious grasp of moral principles – labelled him as disingenuous. The experience of most people was different. He puzzled them a little at first, but they quickly conceived for him a liking and admiration, and these, if they became members of the community of Gresham's, turned often into a deep and affectionate loyalty. As the official head of the school, Howson was an effective figure – strong, earnest, and dignified. But it was in his personal dealings with masters and boys that he was at his best, and we came most truly to appreciate him. We realized how, behind the almost Johnsonian bluntness, there lay an immense kindliness, and a warmth of feeling for his pupils, which made him spontaneously look for the best in them, and, therefore, find it. "Yes, but there is pure gold beneath," was his rebuke, when I passed an impatient criticism on the conduct of a boy in his house; and time taught

Howson's first staff ("The famous five"). Eccles is behind Howson's right shoulder.

me that he was right. Of his affection and sympathy for many of his pupils perhaps only they can speak adequately. "He was a very good father to us," wrote one old boy soon after his death. This simple phrase goes, I think, to the heart of the matter. The longer one knew him the keener was one's impression of a great reserve of power, and of strong impulses sternly schooled.

Although he had a wealth of common sense and great practical wisdom in dealing with the outside world, I always think of him primarily as a man of deep feeling and moral force. It was perfectly true that "he brought something big to the discussion of every subject," but the "something" was usually a generous sentiment or the emphatic and arresting statement of a moral axiom; it was seldom a contribution likely to fall from a man whose power lay first of all in his intellect.

Nobody who worked long under Howson could fail to admire his serenity, and to observe how confidently he faced the inevitable difficulties of his task. He was the last man to be ruffled by petty mishaps, and he was in one sense singularly indifferent to criticism. To criticism of his methods from inside the school he was, it is true, profoundly sensitive; it was disloyalty to the head of the community, striking therefore at the foundation of his work; disloyalty of this kind became more and more the almost unforgivable sin. But for personal criticism from outside he cared not the least. Some might call him pontifical, others, possibly jealous of the school life he had created, might say that his Honour System would produce sneaks or prigs; he went serenely on his way, with absolute confidence in himself and the value of his work.

He presented to his colleagues and pupils a quite extraordinary example of a man devoted to the work of his life, and allowing no competing interests or pleasures to hinder it. His industry was wonderful, and the burden that he took upon himself perhaps excessive, not because he did not know how to delegate, when it was wise to do so, but because he placed no limit to the extent of a head master's or housemaster's personal influence. It was typical of him that, when the war came, he cheerfully undertook the task of trying to keep in touch with every old boy who was serving in the Navy and Army; and there can be no doubt that the labour entailed by this huge correspondence helped to shorten his life. All his energy was directed to the creation of the school. He took no part in local affairs, and kept aloof from current educational controversy and discussion. I think he had a positive dislike of "movements" and "causes," at any rate in the world of education.

It might reasonably be argued that he was unwise in concentrating so closely upon his work, and that both he and his work would have profited, if he had allowed himself more relaxation, and diversity of interest. He would sometimes scarcely leave the school grounds during a whole term, a practice which can have been healthy for neither mind nor body. A lover of Norfolk must indict him for doing a good deal less than justice to the beauty of that corner of the county; he used to say that the country round Holt did not tempt him abroad. Nor did he care greatly for such social life as was open to him in a small country town. There were few professional men living near the school, and Howson was not one to fraternize quite easily with sporting squires and country parsons. He was not a person who could be patronized with impunity, and his opinions about sport and theology were equally unorthodox. "The County," in so far as it was aware of the existence of Gresham's School, apparently had for some time strange ideas about the man who was working there. "That Howson is a terrible Radical, isn't he?" a genial Norfolk sportsman remarked to me not long before I left, and was astonished when I denied the charge. A strange reputation, indeed (for "Radical" in the mouth of a land-owner meant then almost what "Bolshevik" does now) to be borne by one who, during the war, used to say that he would like to see a Carsonian dictatorship!

I do not suppose that misunderstandings of this kind presented any obstacle to Howson's work, for he never desired to base his school upon local support. On the other hand, the emphasis which he placed upon the non-local character of the school certainly

34

made him less popular in the immediate neighbourhood than he might have been otherwise. There are always difficulties when a school, originally founded to meet local requirements, extends its scope, and takes a large proportion of boarders. The jealousy arising in these cases makes an old story in many parts of the country. The parents of day-boys at Gresham's had nothing that could be called a grievance. It is never easy, however, to make day-boys feel that they are getting their fair share of the benefits of a school where the large majority of

The Shooting Team, Bisley (1905)

boys are boarders; and it must be admitted that Howson was not conspicuously successful in this part of his work. The fact is that he was not particularly interested in the problem of how to provide secondary education for the day-boys of a small country town. His work, as he conceived it, was to create a boarding school.

Of those traits in Howson's character that at once influenced and were reflected in the life of the school, one of the most prominent was his dislike of what he conceived to be vulgarity. He felt an intense, and almost morbid, hatred of what was coarse, or ill-bred, or nasty, or "cheap." No man, I should think, ever condemned more severely what may be called conveniently the music-hall type of humour, and the sentiments to which it especially appeals. Who that knew Howson well cannot recall the withering "Isn't that rather poor?" Perhaps in this

Rebuilding Woodlands (1906)

aspect of life, more than in any other, Howson found it difficult to combine hatred of the sin with pity for the sinner. He was sometimes inclined to be hard in his judgment of those whose early life had not been spent in the most refined surroundings.

In place of the second-rate manner of life that he disliked so much, Howson set continually before his boys an alternative ideal of conduct. This he described simply as the "conduct of a gentleman," The last word was often on his lips and he used it, or tried to use it, always with an ethical rather than with a social meaning. I remember him once at Bolton Abbey putting forward the view that the ideas of Christian and of gentleman were in truth the same. Another member of the party, more to start a discussion than for any other reason, asserted that the two ideas were historically and ethically quite different. He found to his surprise that Howson was really hurt by his words, and regretted having uttered them. Howson preached courtesy, because he regarded it as the negation of selfish ness. "Courtesy was a point of honour," wrote someone after his death. The politeness, noticed by visitors as a characteristic of the boys at Holt, was encouraged not as a social trimming, but as the practice of a Christian virtue.

Perhaps I should say *the* Christian virtue. For in Howson's scale of values unselfishness was beyond comparison the most precious of qualities. He used to speak (and who shall say that he was wrong?) as if all that was worst in school life could be described in terms of selfishness – the desire to satisfy one's love of power, or vanity, or sense of ridicule, or animal passions, at the expense of someone else. He had quite as keen an eye for detecting this vice in the greater world. His hatred of what he thought to be selfishness determined his attitude to a good many social and political questions. He was no enemy of private property: but he detested the selfish abuse of it. He had no patience, for example, with local landowners who would not allow his boys to walk in their woods. By temperament he had little sympathy with either the theory or the practice of democracy; but any suggestion of a privilege, jealously guarded, stirred him to a radical indignation.

At one time he was keenly interested in the cause of Women's Suffrage, and his reply, when I once asked him why he supported the movement, was characteristic. "Of course they must have the vote, if they want it. We cannot keep it to ourselves." However much he might sympathize with them on other grounds, he would never give his vote for any group Imperialist, Nationalist, Trade Unionist – if they appeared to be infected with the taint of self-seeking. For that reason, among others, Howson was by no means a good "party man"; he would have thoroughly despised himself if he had been.

In some people this habit of invariably applying the test of altruism would have been rather trying. In Howson it was tolerable, and even admirable, because his creed was exemplified in his life. He was extraordinarily unselfish. I am not thinking only of how he subordinated minor interests and pleasures to the main work of his life. Many men find it easier to be devoted and self-sacrificing in their work than to be considerate "off duty," and unselfish in their amusements. Not so with Howson. Giving, and lending, and thinking for other people, seemed as natural to him in the small things of life as in the great.

I hardly realized this till, some years after I left Holt, I began to join his holiday parties at Bolton Abbey. The ostensible object of these parties was fishing, though some of us went rather to enjoy Howson's conversation, and the sense of belonging once more to the Holt circle. He was an ardent fisherman. He loved the lore of fishing, and, with a delightful inconsistency, he had a good deal of the same boyish fondness for rods and flies that he disliked so much, when it was lavished on cricket bats and golf clubs. He was early on the water in those bleak uninviting days of April that appeal more to an angler's sense of duty than to his hope of catching fish; and the weaker brethren had often finished their tea in front of a blazing fire, before they heard the shuffle of brogued feet on the pathway outside, and saw the burly figure pass the window in the half-light. With all this enthusiasm, he was the most generous of sportsmen. When a limited extent of water had to be divided among too many rods, he was always the most modest in his demands. His first care was to put the least skilful where they would have the most fun; and he would cheerfully give up hours from his own sport to coaching the younger members of his party. Once, when I remonstrated with him for sparing so much time to helping the beginners, he answered in words that were, I believe, absolutely true: "I get as much pleasure from seeing them catch fish as from catching them myself."

A fishing party at Bolton Abbey (Howson at the rear in the hat)

It is tempting, in writing about Howson, to dwell on these fishing holidays, for indeed they meant a great deal to him. He had a wide knowledge of the wet-fly streams of the North, and an intense love of the places where his favourite sport led him. I used to think that there was a special ring in his voice as he pronounced the familiar prayer on Friday mornings: "The changeful glory of sky and sea, of mountain, moor, and river." After trying many places, he found what seemed to him just the right river and quarters for his purpose at Bolton Abbey in Wharfedale. Here in his later years he gathered a party once or twice a year; and here he enjoyed some thing more nearly resembling what most people would call home life than was possible amid the preoccupations of school term. The place gradually acquired for him, as for many others, a wealth of associations. He loved to teach a recruit to his party the names of the different stretches of the river, not only the names in common local use –Sandholmes, and Lobwood, and Waters Meet – but those invented by himself to recall old friends and pupils Richardson's Run, and Barker's Pool, and Cross' Flat.

There is another reason why it seems fitting for me to speak of the holidays I spent with Howson. They gave me an opportunity to observe qualities that were not so easily visible at Holt. I realized, for example, his power of rapid, concentrated, work. He would sit down calmly in a crowded room, and in a few minutes write half a dozen of his terse vigorous letters, each one involving a decision of some moment, apparently quite oblivious of the general conversation. He showed, too, on these occasions an infectious buoyancy and gaiety of spirit that I had only suspected to exist, when I knew him solely as my head master. By 1908, when the school had grown to a considerable size, and his position was one of some prominence, he did not in public often feel able to put off "the head master." But in his own house, at his own table in hall, with old boys, and with his constant succession of guests, he could still sometimes reveal a sympathy with high spirits, that must have been invaluable in the earliest days, when the school was only a kind of enlarged family party.

One incident that I can remember happening at Bolton may be worth recording. A stranger had arrived at the hotel, and getting into conversation with Howson, had presently disclosed the fact that he was looking for a school for his youngest son.

J. H. Simpson, artist, fisherman and dog owner

"Where are you thinking of sending him?" asked someone. "To Holt," replied the unsuspecting stranger, not having the least idea who Howson was. "Why to Holt?" asked the latter, interested and amused. "Because my other two boys who are at ... (mentioning the name of a well-known public school) tell me that the Holt boys are the best behaved at camp." The responsibility of an O.T.C. contingent for the good name of their school was a favourite theme of Howson's, and I could see that he was delighted by this unexpected testimony to the conduct of his boys.

. . . .

Character, as shown in a certain standard of conduct, was what he aimed at always, and he seems never to have doubted that, for all but a few boys, this standard was attainable. He had, indeed, a far firmer belief than most schoolmasters of his generation in the "goodness" of human nature. A boy seemed to him to be educable to almost any extent. But this could only take place through his close personal contact with adults, who would mould his character by showing him right standards. Quite definitely Howson thought of his work as that of moulding character from without, rather than of allowing the opportunity of growth from within.

One of the sharpest impressions left with his boys was that the *whole of conduct* in every detail of speech and action was important, and not parts of it only. He hated the division of life (whether for the individual or for the community) into "water-tight compartments." He knew that in school life details often count most. "In those early days," wrote his second-master, " he had the insight – and it was here that his genius partly lay – to see what were the things, often very small and apparently insignificant, which would ultimately produce far-reaching results." One might quote as an example the emphasis that he placed upon punctuality. At first it seemed rather exaggerated; to be late for a lesson was to be guilty of something really discreditable. Yet looking back I can see that the anxiety to be punctual for every engagement, and the feeling that to be late was to be selfish and ill-mannered, counted for a good deal in promoting the busy, purposeful, and considerate behaviour that Howson valued so highly. Nobody could say that the moral ideal so continuously set before his boys was an easy one to express in terms of school life. He aimed high; and the best proof of his greatness as a head master lies in the fact that his aim was realized. In this respect he compares favourably with some educational reformers, men with wider reputations, and in some cases a stronger taste for publicity. There have been headmasters whose ideas were more original than Howson's, whose theoretical knowledge was greater, and

Howson and the boys of School House (1905)

whose imaginative reach was wider. Unfortunately the closest observers have too often noticed a disappointing divergence between what they aspire to and what they achieve. Howson not only initiated ideas; he translated them into action, so that they permeated the life of the community. His moral code, so far from being an easy one, would have been deemed by most people to be impracticable for boys. It made large demands on their loyalty and self-control, and few allowances for

43

the vagaries of youth. "Boys will be boys" was answered summarily, if not very scientifically, by Howson with "Why should they not be men?" Yet it is true that the code of conduct which he preached was, in fact, the code accepted and observed by the school. To bring about this result, he used all the authority of his position as head master, and all the force of his character. The life of the school centered round his personality. Boys quickly knew whether he approved or disapproved, and the knowledge decided their conduct. "It did matter above all things," to quote one of the truest remarks ever made about Holt, "what the head master thought of you." What he thought of you depended upon whether he regarded you as "helpful," that is to say, as loyally upholding the moral standard. In comparison with this, everything else was relatively unimportant. Life at Gresham's was many-sided, and every kind of healthy interest was encouraged. But there were no *imperia in imperio*, with separate aims and standards of their own. No other excellence or enthusiasm atoned for a rebellious or indifferent attitude to the intense, if rather narrow, convictions that decided Howson's outlook upon the moral function of the school.

In so far as religion can be separated from morality, it may be said that he subordinated the former to the latter. With regard to the part played by religion in school life, he believed (if one may compare small things with great) in the "State Church," rather than the "Free Church in the Free State." He was the very opposite of a sacerdotalist, and the clerical members of the staff, apart from conducting the services, had no greater influence than the laymen on the religious life of the boys. "What's wrong with this school," remarked a disagreeable visitor in quite early days, "is that the laymen are trying to be parsons, and the parsons trying to be laymen." If he had heard this criticism, Howson would not have been at all worried. Of theology, as of philosophy, he was as impatient as he was ignorant. Masters and boys who discussed religious questions with him were sometimes surprised at what seemed the vagueness of his views. The Anglican clergyman who called him a "devout pagan" was probably smarting from the effect of a salutary snub; but it was easy to see what he meant. If by religion is meant the conscious implicit adherence to a particular creed, there have been many more religious men than Howson. But in the value of what some people call "practical religion" – the attempt to live according to Christian ethics – he had a constant and radiant faith.

In comparison with moral worth, intellectual excellence counted with Howson for little. Academic successes reflecting credit upon the school pleased him for that reason, but he never overestimated the importance of university scholarships and similar honours. As time went on, these came in a goodly number. Natural science and mathematics brought the first successes, but the humanist subjects soon followed, and Howson lived to see his school winning at least its full share of university honours. These results were in no way surprising. He aimed as little as any man at examination successes; but in a school where it was good form to work hard and to have plenty of interests, brains were bound to have a fine chance of showing what they could do. His system prepared a good soil in the intellectual field, though he wisely left the cultivation of it to others.

On the whole it may be said that Howson was not really interested in the purely academic side of school work. He distrusted the merely "clever" boy, and he detested anything approaching pedantry. When he went to Holt, he had certain convictions about what a curriculum should be, and these he immediately put into practice. French was to be taught, so far as was possible, by conversation, there was to be plenty of mathematics and natural science, in the form of physics and chemistry, and the classics were to be kept in the background.

For the time being he seems to have been fairly content with that, and in 1908 the curriculum of the school was still badly lopsided. The humanities were relatively neglected, and later reforms, remedying this fault, were made principally on the initiative of his colleagues. Howson himself was not a widely read man, and his attitude to the literary side of education was sometimes rather trying. "Biography," I heard him once remark to an astonished man of letters, who was visiting the school, "why, that is almost as dull as history!" A strange judgment to be passed by one who was so intensely interested in his living fellow men! By removing, or subordinating, the teaching of Greek and Latin he believed that he had freed his boys from a great incubus. No doubt there was much to be said for this view, so far as it applied to the mass of meaningless grammatical drill, which was the bane of classical teaching thirty or forty years ago. But I think it is better to admit that there was in Howson's attitude to the classics a good deal of honest human prejudice and "rationalisation." The classical scholar, as a type, stood to him for what was reactionary in education, and he was rather inclined to dismiss his learning as pedantry. Latin, therefore, was made an alternative subject, with no superfluous time allotted to it, and there was no Greek taught, except in so far as it had to be "crammed" for examinations. In a school so mentally active in many directions, the lack of classical culture for the abler boys was less calamitous than it would have been in a more torpid atmosphere. But one was sometimes conscious of the loss. It was a shock to hear an old boy, who had been in the sixth form, talk about "Homer and the other Latin poets." It would have been interesting to see the result of giving a fair chance to subjects that inevitably demand a certain amount of drudgery, in a school where the standard of industry was so high. One very pleasing and educative feature of Gresham's was the prominence given to music. Howson loved music himself, and his experience at Uppingham, which had for many years a high musical reputation, probably taught him what part it could play in school life. He gave unusual facilities for the study of music in school hours, and under exceptionally happy and gifted direction the music of Gresham's became not merely a barely tolerated "side-show," or the amiable accomplishment of a few unusual boys, but a creative influence felt by nearly all. For one kind of excellence, atoning at some schools for almost every sin, Howson had little regard. He had a most salutary contempt for the athletic grandee, and could not see why he should be

The Chapel, Gresham's School

treated differently from anyone else. I remember telling him a remark I had overheard, while watching a cricket match at a great public school. At a critical time one of the school bowlers, a boy who had been lately guilty of rather serious misconduct, was dismissing the opposition side by some excellent bowling. His radiant housemaster pushed up to a colleague with the words: "I think even the head master will forgive him now." I suppose most of us would regard the words as stupid. To

47

Howson they must have seemed the words of an imbecile.

He regarded games and athletics as healthy and agreeable exercise – nothing more. Anything tending to give them a fictitious importance, whether in school or in the world outside, particularly if it in any way encouraged professionalism, he considered ridiculous or mischievous. He was very severe on all sporting journalism and on the weaker brethren, who open their daily paper at the cricket news. Indeed, his indifference

A Physical Science Laboratory

to what, after all, matters of interest to the great majority of our fellow citizens, was sometimes rather disconcerting. I remember being asked, with some of my colleagues, to meet at dinner a rather distinguished visitor to the School House. "Bad news from Australia, isn't it?" had begun the latter in a harmless attempt to make conversation, when he was brought up short by Howson's blank expression. It would be difficult to say which was the more surprised, the guest at finding a public schoolmaster who did not know that a Test Match was in progress, or his host at the idea of anyone of intelligence sparing a thought for so trivial a matter.

As commonly happened, when Howson felt strongly on any subject, his keen dislike of exaggerated athleticism was reflected in the rules of the school and the general atmosphere. Nothing was allowed that could tempt boys to attach a false value to games. He expressed his opinion on the subject strongly and frequently, and everyone knew that the kind of boy who was always talking and thinking about games was not the kind most approved by those in authority. Prominence in games, for example, counted for very little when prefects were chosen. As a result, Gresham's was entirely free from that rather pathetic figure the athletic "blood," and the boys spent far less time than at most schools talking and reading about games. I cannot remember seeing the lemon-coloured back and plump body of a "Wisden" during the whole of my time at Holt. Perhaps the orthodox games-master would have thought that the legitimate sphere of games was sometimes unfairly invaded. I can remember my own conventional prejudices receiving a shock, when I saw a boy summoned to the head master's study from the field of play, while cock-house match was actually in progress, or heard that a boy was not allowed to receive his "eleven" colours, because he was in one of the lowest forms. Yet it was things like this that prevented the creation of "watertight compartments."

Howson's treatment of games is a good example of how, by insisting upon apparent details (whether by way of command or prohibition), he obtained a wider result. There were no cups or other athletic trophies, and "colours" were reduced to a minimum. Howson had no taste for the usual athletic millinery. This, unless it is carefully watched, always tends to increase.

For years the boys were forbidden to shout when watching football matches, and ordered to confine their applause to the clapping of hands. The familiar starter's pistol and the "scrum-cap" were both taboo. Undoubtedly these measures made some people restive, particularly the veto on matches against other schools; but many, who know what the worship of games can become, will applaud Howson's wisdom in setting his face from the start against the first signs of an insidious evil.

It will, perhaps, by now be plain that his methods demanded implicit loyalty to the school, and that he wanted boys to feel the moral code of Gresham's to be almost the biggest thing in their lives. This code was not one for term time only. No head master could have recognized more deeply than did Howson the value of home influence. He touched constantly on the subject in his addresses. He was one of those who can speak to boys in public about a mother's influence with real tenderness, and without making them feel mawkish and unmanly. Few who heard it will forget his moving sermon on "Home Letters." Yet he was the last man to let a boy believe that "my people allow me to do it at home" was necessarily the final word on any question of conduct. He used, for example, to ask his school prefects not to smoke in the holidays, whatever view their parents might have in the matter. Probably, too, it was some feeling that Gresham boys should be guided in their mutual relations by the Gresham code, and by no competing standard of loyalty, that made him always inclined to dislike the practice of boys staying with each other in the holidays

. . . . .

I have tried to give some impression of Howson's personality, and the Ideal that he kept before him in making the school. But I have hardly yet considered the actual points of contact between him and the boys, and his means of influencing them.

50

His Honour System comprised two mutually interdependent aspects – the peculiar personal relation between a boy and his housemaster, and what may be called the general spirit of responsibility and loyalty. The former, of course, helped to create the latter, but there were other contributing factors.

Every head master must to some extent influence his boys through his staff. Except in the case of housemasters, this applies less to Howson than to many head masters; but there can be no

Swedish Drill at Gresham's

question of the effect produced on the boys by the standard of duty and efficiency demanded by Howson of his masters, and for the most part willingly and even enthusiastically observed by them. I have said that to be a master at Gresham's could be an extraordinarily happy experience; but the happiness depended almost entirely upon whether you enjoyed your work, and were prepared to devote yourself to it whole-heartedly. If Howson trusted a man, and believed him to be loyal to himself, and to the school, he would allow him the widest freedom with regard to teaching, and lend a ready ear to his suggestions. It was surprising, for example, how ready he was as a housemaster to listen to a young master's comments upon boys in his house. But he was not one to pamper his staff, or to let them think that their personal convenience or private interests mattered very much to him, in comparison with the smooth running of the school. He did not at all favour exchanges of lessons, or week-ends away from the school. Nor had he much patience with people who missed lessons owing to trifling indispositions. When serious illness came, Howson was wholly kind and sympathetic, but from minor ailments he expected others to be as free as he kept himself. He had many sound ideas about health, not least that illness – especially epidemic illness – is increased by thinking and talking about it. Fussiness he regarded as almost criminal.

The young master learned a good deal about Howson's point of view from the periodical masters' meetings. Here discussion often ranged beyond details of routine to questions of principle, and I have always thought that the head master brought up points for discussion more as a means of educating his staff, then because he wanted to arrive at a collective judgment. He never felt bound to discuss important decisions, if he preferred not to do so, and he had a most admirable power of keeping his own counsel. He was easily accessible, too, to his colleagues in other less formal ways. The unfailing hospitality of the School House always made us feel welcome, and we never visited him in his study for a private talk without finding him ready to listen patiently. Howson was not one to press his advice unasked, but to some of us; from being merely the trusted and sympathetic head master, he became the wise counsellor in affairs quite outside of work in the school. There are others of his colleagues, beside myself, who will remember how he could kindle hope and courage in days of personal difficulty or sorrow.

With regard to his other means of contact with the boys, he

believed, in the first place, that it was part of a head master's duty to know directly every boy in the school, and that no school should be too large for this to be the case. I have heard him repeatedly say that he would not be comfortable as head of a school where this personal contact was impossible. He had placed a definite limit, beyond which he did not wish Gresham's to grow. In 1908 there were three senior houses and one junior house; another senior house was added later. Some people who

Howson and his staff (1908)

knew Gresham's well, and admired Howson's work there, used to say that he would be a failure as head master of a school of five or six hundred boys. I am by no means sure that they were right. But it is true that in such a position he would have been compelled radically to alter his methods.

Though he had more than nominal knowledge of every boy in

School Prefects (1901)

the school, his closest relations were naturally with his own house. He disliked the idea of the head master of a boarding school not having a house. In his own case, he trusted the schoolhouse to present a working model of his ideal school. I have heard him say that the boys of a head master's house should be "missionaries of his ideas." This is a policy not without danger. It might, and I think it sometimes did, place

54

the members of his own house in a somewhat invidious light. Schoolboy society does not always discriminate between the youthful "missionary" and the youthful prig. This was, I think, the real trouble on those occasions (happily not many) when the relations between the senior houses were not so friendly as Howson would have liked them to be. To the general danger of excessive "house feeling," especially in a school consisting of only a few boarding houses, Howson was fully alive, and, in comparison with many schools Gresham's was singularly free from it. This was due not only to Howson's outspoken condemnation of the evil but to the loyalty of his housemasters, and the influence that he exercised over his school prefects. The latter were chosen from the leading boys of all houses.

Some kind of prefect system has become part of the tradition of English boarding schools, and Howson, like other head masters, delegated some of his authority to prefects. For a number of reasons, however, the prefects at Holt exercised less official power, particularly of a punitive kind, than those of most public schools. In a school where the individual boy was directly related to his head master, or house master, by the Honour System the authority of the prefect was less needed. All Howson's views, too, were opposed to granting the prefects any considerable power of punishment. He observed two main principles with regard to prefects. They were to be "leaders" and not "policemen," and they were to be chosen for their character and loyalty. Roughly speaking, there have been two recognized systems of selecting prefects, the sixth form system (which was Arnold's), and the system of selection according to individual character. In practice the latter has two dangers. It often plays into the hands of the athleticists, so that the prefects are merely those who are good at games; and masters may be tempted to choose those who will make things run smoothly and give them quiet lives, without bothering very much about the methods which their henchmen employ. The whole spirit of

Gresham's made these dangers negligible.

If Howson allowed his prefects less than the usual degree of disciplinary power he believed that they could be of the greatest value through their personal influence and example. His *school* prefects, in particular, were to be shining examples of right conduct. Their tie of loyalty to himself was particularly close. It is worth while to quote some words spoken on one of the early Arbor Days, quaint ceremonies, I have been told (for they had ceased to exist by 1908), at which prominent boys were invited to plant trees, as a memorial of their service to the school. "In our prefects," he said, "we look for unflinching straightforwardness, desperate earnestness, and untarnished honour." To become a school prefect meant for most boys a real self-discipline, and I believe that in some cases the strain was almost too severe. Be that as it may, Howson's confidence in his school prefects was rarely misplaced.

Naturally members of the School House saw most of the head master, but all boys came in contact with him in the weekly lesson that he gave to every form. One gathers that to be present at one of these lessons was often a remarkable experience. Howson did not excel as a class teacher of a subject. His French was not first-rate, and his geography certainly did not accord with modern methods. He regarded his lessons, especially his scripture lessons, frankly as an opportunity for discussing any conceivable subject, if he thought it might usefully be ventilated, and for taking soundings in the public opinion of the school. Sometimes, if he was in the mood, he would propound all manner of questions of major and minor ethics, invite opinions, and allow a surprising freedom of discussion. No doubt everybody was not equally courageous on these occasions; in certain directions, at any rate, it was not regarded as expedient to be too outspoken. But any form of discussion was not without value. At other times Howson

56

would denounce some error of principle or taste, ranging from the most serious moral problems, to the colour of ties or socks. His catholicity in choice of subjects did not please everyone, I remember an irate member of the sixth form complaining that his scripture lesson had consisted, in hearing Howson read aloud an article from the Spectator on Syndicalism. His lessons were certainly unorthodox. It is difficult to believe that they were ever uninteresting, for sooner or later they were bound to touch shrewdly and intimately upon one of those points of

Arbor Day (1902)

school ethics that stirred Howson's enthusiasm or indignation.

The fact was that in these weekly lessons the boys heard from Howson the same message, though with more detailed application, that they heard when he was preaching on Sunday evening, or addressing the assembled school after prayers on a weekday morning. On these last occasions Howson was at his very best. In a few impressive sentences, without wasting

57

a word, he would point the moral of some recent event or bestow merited praise, or treat incisively and scornfully a deed which he thought was unworthy of the doer and his school. He had a wonderful power of identifying himself with what was best in his audience, so that he appeared to be expressing *their* will rather than to be imposing *his* will upon them. As an old boy wrote to me, "he gave the *impression* (quite false) of a self-governing community with himself as head with supreme veto." Thus, when he was finding fault, the offenders seemed to be isolated from public sympathy, rather than to be supported by it. One comparatively small instance of this used to occur after prayers on weekday mornings. If any article had been found lying about in the corridors or classrooms, Howson would hold it up, and the owner would bashfully walk up before the whole school, and claim it. At many schools it would have been generally felt that it was "bad luck" on the culprit to be made thus conspicuous. I never noticed that sentiment at Holt. Everyone seemed to take it for granted that, if you were careless, you deserved to be made to appear rather foolish.

It was the same when he had to express his displeasure in more serious matters. Without apparent effort he won public opinion to his side. He never pleaded with his hearers, or scolded, or nagged, or "talked down" to them. He spoke with a quiet confidence in the truth of the appeal that he was making, and in their power and will to respond to it.

It was this that made his sermons so impressive. Nothing is easier – or less profitable-than to pick holes in a sermon and Howson's sermons were, no doubt, in some respects open to criticism. In literary form they were far from flawless, and he had some unfortunate tricks of intonation, "She always tells me not to whine;" he said to me of an outspoken lady, "do I whine?" His quotations, too, were not always pleasing. He was too ready to interrupt his own simple and sincere language with a passage from some tiresome American divine, or a tag from a well-known hymn. I do not know how far these minor faults weighed with most of his hearers. For my own part, after a fairly wide experience of school chapels, and having listened to a good many men who have been used to addressing boys, I consider Howson's sermons as far the best and most impressive school sermons I have ever heard. They gained, I am sure, in power from their comparative infrequency. He seldom, if ever, preached more than once a term, and his sermons were an outstanding event awaited with interest. He was able, too, to speak to his small school with greater intimacy than If he had been addressing five or six hundred boys The power of his sermons, however, lay In the fact that they were essentially *school sermons*. They were not theology made easy, nor introductions to social problems, nor clever essays in Biblical criticism, but earnest and sympathetic efforts to help schoolboys in the problems encountered in their personal life at school. And they were delivered with the deep sincerity of a man who was more interested in those problems than in anything else in the world. He possessed, too, one of the rarest gifts in a school preacher – the power to make his sermons appeal equally to the older and to the younger boys.

. . . .

In these various ways Howson put before the boys his conception of right and wrong, and thereby produced what I have called the general spirit of Gresham's "Rule of Life" would almost be a correct description, for Holt naturally recalls some of those historic communities, which have separated themselves from the world to live according to a rule of their own. It was a morality that looked always to the welfare of the community, insisting at the same time that this could be attained only through a sense of responsibility and self-respect of every individual. On the responsibility of each boy for others

– especially in friendship – he dwelt often. I doubt if there was ever a school where even the youngest and newest boys felt so vividly that not only masters or senior boys, but they too themselves, could help to make their school good or bad. The appeal to every boy's self-respect was not only, or primarily, verbal. It lay in the fact that he was trusted. By releasing him from the old tyranny of rules, and "bounds," and penalties Howson had shown a belief in the boy's capacity to remain true to the best in his nature.

When, however, I say that a boy was "trusted," I feel that some further explanation is necessary. In his idea of what trust means, and his way of putting it into practice, Howson differed from other schoolmasters. In one sense, no doubt, the public schools themselves are based on the principle of trust, for, though the younger boys are hedged in by innumerable restrictions, the prefects are usually allowed a much wider liberty, and are expected to co-operate with the masters in enforcing the regulations of the school. Even the younger boys, especially in a school where every boy has a study, are allowed to spend a good many hours of the day free from active supervision. Indeed, when a master says that he trusts his boys, he commonly means that he lets them alone. They know how they are expected to behave, and he assumes that they will do so. Further, he will act on this assumption, even though he suspects, or knows, that his trust is sometimes abused, and that he cannot always rely upon hearing of this abuse, when it occurs. The traditional "schoolboy honour" is bound, as he well knows, to keep him to some extent in the dark. Still for quite definite reasons he holds it best, until an actual offender is discovered, to *appear* to believe that his confidence is not misplaced. He knows, in the first place, that the other moral influences and general discipline of the school are helping him progressively; that a boy who is at first unreliable may in course of time grow to be trustworthy. But, far more important, he believes that the evil

Day boys catching the train

of occasional failures is outweighed by the good that comes from boys thinking that they are trusted; a few failures are a lesser evil than general suspicion on the part of the master, and dependence on the part of the boys.

Howson thought of it all rather differently. As I said earlier, his belief in the possibilities of a boy's nature was far higher than that of most men. He denied the inevitability of failures. But his whole system demanded that a boy should not be left alone, but should be in closest possible touch with adult influence. This influence could be exercized in many different ways; some of these I have already mentioned, and some of them are in no sense peculiar to Holt. There were certain matters, however, that in Howson's opinion were particularly decisive in the development of character, and the growth of good "tone" in the school. In these, he decided that there must be something more than the usual safeguards against evil. There must be a definite compact, or understanding, between master and boy, binding the boy not only – or perhaps I should say, not so much – to restrain himself from the offences in question, but to tell the master, if his power of self-restraint failed him. Thus there would be no danger of either of Howson's bugbears, a "fool's paradise" on one side, or a "conspiracy of silence" on the other. The compact itself might cover only a comparatively small sphere. Howson felt that the high standard produced in that sphere, and the habit of intimate talk between the boy and his housemaster would spread from that sphere to cover the whole field of conduct. To put it in a different way – a compact, which in certain particulars was *expressed*, would be felt to be generally *implied*.

This private compact was the core of Howson's Honour System. He believed it to be responsible for everything that was most distinctive at Holt. It is not easy, however, to describe accurately what happened, for the method was not rigid and stereotyped, but essentially human, and personal, and varied to meet individual cases. I believe this point to have been essential to his system and it explains both why it was equally effective with many types of boy, and why it is possible to hear it described quite differently by different people. I have heard it said that the Honour System was never worked properly except in two houses, and it was liable to be modified in these. I can hope to describe only the essential features of a system that was continually developing.

The head master interviewed all new boys soon after their arrival, and spoke shortly about the moral ideals of the school. He asked the boys if they would enter into a compact, that they would not themselves indulge, and would try to prevent others indulging, in three things, smoking, swearing, and indecency (interpreting the last in its widest sense). If a boy said "Yes" (he nearly always did) he was told to give this assurance to his housemaster. The latter was thus given an opportunity of talking frankly to each boy on the subject or morals, sexual and otherwise, and establishing a further mutual understanding. It was an essential part of the compact that if the boy failed to keep his promise in any of these three respects, he should "own up."

It may seem at first that to speak of a "compact" is misleading, for all the undertaking was apparently on one side. But what Howson undertook (not, of course, in so many words, but in the whole spirit of his work) was vastly important. It was nothing less than that he would treat these and any other schoolboy misdemeanours in a way quite different from that of the traditional schoolmaster, not as a criminal judge, but as a sympathetic father. It is one thing to report your failure to a man bound to visit them with impositions, the birch, or even expulsion. It is quite a different matter to confess to a man who will meet you with sternness, perhaps, but always with understanding and encouragement. Of one thing there can be no possible doubt, and it applies both to the Honour System itself, and to the relations of boys with their housemaster arising from it. Many Greshamians felt at the time that these confessions and intimate conversations were not only the basis of all that was best in the school life, but were the greatest help to them individually. They held that they were thereby strengthened and encouraged in dealing with the usual problems of boyhood – not least with the autoerotic and other sexual disturbances common in adolescence. To them, at any rate, the idea of a moral supervision, extending to the most intimate details of their private lives, was not an incubus but a comfort.

Beyond doubt, the system provokes criticism, and raises the most searching questions. It is in conflict in many respects with public school orthodoxy. It is a challenge to those who think that the worst educational sin is to prolong dependence upon adult authority beyond the age of childhood. My present object, however, is not to answer theoretical criticism, but to describe how the system worked in practice. I will add only such explanation as I think necessary in order to avoid certain dangerous misapprehensions. I will deal first with the feature of the system most obnoxious to the ordinary public school-man, the boy's obligation in the last resort to report an offender to the authorities. Let me say at once that in practice the need very seldom arose. Discussion of what the obligation meant is, therefore, rather unreal; but theoretically, at least, it meant this: If you heard or saw anything wrong, and knew that a boy had definitely broken his promise, you reminded the offender that he ought to report himself; after an interval, if nothing happened, and he still *positively refused to do so*, you reported the matter yourself to the captain of the house; the latter then used his influence to try to persuade the offender to "own up"; and only if he too was unsuccessful, was the matter taken directly to the housemaster.

Another point has troubled some critics, though, in comparison with the larger issues involved, it hardly appears to me to need much attention. It seems at first sight to show a strange scale of moral values to pick out two or three quite different offences for similar treatment, and thereby place them, as it were, on an equality. Howson's answer, when I once put this point to him, was that if a boy became accustomed to the practice of "owning up" in the less serious case, he would find it less difficult to do so if the graver occasion arose. I think his reply fairly met the criticism and later on he removed one possibility of any serious confusion of thought, by taking swearing out of the list of offences.

64

Waiting for the train at Weybourne Station

One aspect of Howson's work, intimately connected with
this matter of promises and confessions, must be noticed
again briefly, though to be adequately considered it would
require a treatise in itself. I refer to his treatment of the sexual
impulses and difficulties of the adolescent boy. No doubt many
psychologists would hold that the problem is often far more
subtle than Howson realized. Sexual abnormality and over-
tension may be, indirectly at least, the result of early repression
and dependence. A system that is continually emphasizing an
obligation of the boy to admit adult influence and supervision
over the whole area of his life, may in such cases be reinforcing
the deepest, because the unconscious, causes of the mischief.
All this may be true, and yet the fact remains that in this matter
Howson was ahead of most of his contemporaries. He used
frank explanation and encouragement instead of blame. For
the vague idea of "vice" he substituted one that was healthier
and saner. He never allowed sexual misdemeanours to put him

in a panic. And he believed that expulsion for moral failure, like superannuation for academic failure, was often a cowardly device for enabling a head master to escape his duty.

The Honour System, indeed, as worked by Howson, is best thought of as a means of giving the housemaster endless opportunities of privately encouraging his boys, and enlisting their help on his side. It would be a great mistake to think that, because the boy promised not to do certain things, the Honour System was something negative. It was effective in its preventive work. Many common features of public school life (some of them not after all so very wicked) were not to be found at Holt. It may have been true that as an old Greshamian once flippantly said to me "Gresham's was the only school where your maiden aunt could live for a term without being shocked." But the real strength of the Honour System lay not in what it *prevented*, but in what it created. It brought into being, as I have already said, a wonderfully keen sense, in even the junior boy, that he was co-operating with his housemaster and the older boys in fixing the "tone" of the school. The Honour System was certainly highly successful in making everyone feel that he had a moral "stake in the country."

The strength of the system, at its best, probably lay in the fact that it appealed to two complementary sides of a boy's nature. It appealed to his loyalty to the master, who represented adult authority and tradition. It appealed, also, to his more enterprising side. He knew perfectly well that his school was still young, with its place in the world yet to be won. By playing his part loyally he was taking his share, though it might be a comparatively humble one, in an adventure conducted by a trusted and inspiring leader.

I recognize that this account of the Honour System is sadly imperfect. Perhaps the word "system" is itself misleading, when

"The School House Five". (1903)

applied to anything so essentially personal and unfettered as Howson's relations with his school. Such a subtle relationship is not easy to describe. Judging from past experience, I am prepared to believe that my attempt to reproduce something of the atmosphere of Gresham's will be less unsuccessful with the general reader than with members of my own profession. I have usually found (and others tell me that they have found the same thing) that to talk to schoolmasters, at any rate masters at public schools, about Holt is to encounter one of two replies. Either a polite incredulity is expressed that the place, as I have described it, could exist; or there comes the complacent and rather irritating answer that "after all Howson was only doing what we are all trying to do ourselves, without his opportunity." Both these comments are more interesting subjectively than as serious criticism, but a word must be said about each.

With regard to the first, incredulity must give way to plain evidence. Everyone will not, of course, agree with every detail of my description of Gresham's, but I cannot imagine anyone in a position to judge, who will not agree that the life there was strikingly different from that of other schools. I will not pretend that there were no failures, or that everyone always lived up to Howson's standards, wonderfully well as they were usually observed. Howson, too, would have been more than human, if he had not sometimes been tempted to pitch his estimate of the school ethics rather too high. One can hardly, for instance, take

The 1903 wrought iron gates off the Cromer Road. The left hand crest is of the Fishmongers' Company and on the right, those of the founder, Sir John Gresham.

literally a passage in one of his published sermons where he tells his hearers to be "proud of your tradition that two hundred boys can and ought to live together without the interchange of a low word or a base deed, and that weeks and months and years pass without a break of this splendid tradition." Such occasional exaggeration was pardonable. I maintain that nobody with an intimate knowledge of the school could return anything but a negative answer, to the half-ironical question that Howson sometimes put to his prefects and old boys: "Am I living in a fool's paradise?"

The longer one knew the school, the more one realized that there was nothing superficial in its obvious loyalty to the head master and his standards. It is possible, no doubt, to imagine a school where the boys might be made to behave much as did the boys at Gresham's, but only at the cost of a great deal of underlying resentment and disloyalty. That was not at all true of Holt. Some boys, of course, caught the spirit of the place more quickly and easily than others; some boys, as at all schools with a distinctive character, never "understood" at all, but took everything for granted. From time to time there may have been boys who were, or pretended to be restive at not being "more like other public schools." But the public opinion created by Howson never approved, and barely tolerated, the professed rebel. There was not a grain of hero-worship for the opponent of authority.

The second criticism that I have mentioned means, no doubt, in the first place, that the attempted explanation has failed to carry conviction. It implies, also, a curious disbelief in the possibility of achieving what may be called broadly public-school ends, by other than the orthodox public-school means. In one sense it may be admitted, the end pursued by all honest schoolmasters is the same. But Gresham's school departed in some respects so sharply from the accepted type, as to imply a new and different scale of moral values. I am not contending for the moment that it was *better* or *worse* than the great public schools at their best; but it was certainly quite different. To schoolmasters who would say that Howson's work was not markedly original, I am inclined to put the following questions:

Are you prepared so to organize and govern your school, that *moral* excellence comes always and everywhere first? Moral,

69

I mean, according to adult standards? In comparison with this, will you allow athletic excellence, and even intellectual excellence, to count practically for nothing? This will affect not only your games and school matches, but your whole prefect system, and your choice of masters.

Are you prepared practically to abolish the distinction between sin and crime, and to treat "breaches of discipline" as faults to be visited with displeasure, but not with punishment?

Are you prepared to use as your chief instrument *personal loyalty*? To be a "father," with all the responsibilities thereby entailed? To have it said of you that it matters to a boy more than anything else what you think of him?

Each of these questions raises issues that allow the greatest divergence of opinion. Howson never tried to evade them, and he faced his responsibility with courage and faith. To the convictions formed, for the most part, before he went to Holt, or soon after his arrival, he remained true to the end. It was no small part of his strength that he was so sure of his own mind. He was no fanatic. He held his educational creed sanely and tolerantly. He was always eager to hear of other original work in education, and quick to appreciate its merit. Anything like jealousy was utterly foreign to him. But he knew the value of what he had himself created, and he was immensely proud of the old boys, who were the living evidence of his work. He never attempted to hide his belief – a belief held without the slightest arrogance or complacency – that Gresham's stood for a nobler conception of boyhood than he had found elsewhere.

Appendix

"A Nest of Singing Birds"

B ....Bengal Lodge
F.....................Farfield
H ....School House, Howson's
K ....Kenwyn
o ....Old School House, Junior
OSH.................Old School House
W ....Woodlands

Sir John Reith (1889-1971, B 1904-06) was the son of a
Scottish Free Church
minister. After school
where he did not work
hard but enjoyed games he
was sent as an engineering
apprentice to Glasgow. He
joined the BBC in 1922 at
its inception and rose to be
its first Director General.
A combination of his father's and Howson's moral fervour
enabled him quickly to set the high moral tone of the BBC and
to establish its traditions, not least of giving equal consideration
to all view points, but his invariable high moral stance did not
endear him to everyone. In the war he worked at first for the
Government but he and Churchill did not get on. Churchill
once said of him, 'There stalks that wuthering height'. (He was
6ft 7ins!) The Reith Lectures were established in his honour
in 1948. Directorships and honours followed after the war but
he died a disappointed man. The Reith Science Building was
named after him and as a governer of the school he opened the
new administrative building.

Lesley Everett Baynes (1902-89, o 1912-14) 'learned his engineering skills at school and in industry.' His first patent was in 1919 (aged 17) a variable pitch air screw. He was later responsible for the aerodynamic design of the first Singapore flying boat. During the war he designed guided missiles from submarines for the RAF. He also designed the SCUD sailplane (glider). After it he invented and built the first high lift (vertical takeoff) research aircraft, then he designed and patented the variable sweep (swing wing) aircraft and the high speed hydrofoil sea craft. A room in the Gresham's Design centre is dedicated to him.

GOOD BUSINESS.—Mr. Baynes illustrating special features of the "Scud," four of which have now been sold at the Glider Exhibition by E. D. Abbott Ltd.

Three **Spender** brothers: **Michael Spender** (1906-45, H 1917-25.) was in the same form as W. H. Auden. They both went to Oxford as scientists, Michael as a scholar of Balliol College. He was a leading figure in the interpretation of aerial photography in the Second World War and was killed in an air-crash at the end of it.

Sir Stephen Spender (1909-95, OSH 1918-19), poet, critic

and broadcaster. He met Auden at Oxford and became a lifelong friend. He was co-editor of *Encounter*, Professor of English at University College, London and a distinguished writer. He gave the Valedictory address at Auden's Memorial Service in Christ Church and edited the tributes to him.

Humphrey Spender (1910-2005, H 1924-29) was a photographic journalist, textile designer and painter. After the war he was a tutor at the Royal College of Art and took groundbreaking pictures for *Picture Post*. He and Ben Nicholson knew each other well.

All three **Nicholson** brothers were in Woodlands. **Ben** (1894-1982, W 1909), withdrawn from the Removes, for reasons of ill-health / overwork. He suffered frequently all his life from asthma. He played successfully for the 1st XI cricket for which he received his colours blazer. He went straight on to The Slade School of Art, where he studied for one year. He was a leading light of the British modern movement and was married to Winifred Nicholson and later, Barbara Hepworth, both artists of importance. Before the Second World War he forged links with

Ben Nicholson

members of the *avant-garde* movement in Paris. After it he was a key figure in the influential art colony in St Ives, Cornwall. He won virtually all the international prizes available. **John Anthony** (Tony) (1897-1918, W 1909-14.) He went to Gresham's at the same time as his elder brother. They were known as Nicholson Major and Minor. He was killed in the last months of the 1914-18 war. **Christopher** (Kit) (1904-48, W 1919-23) was the leading architect in the incipient modern movement in the years before the war and was an International Gliding Champion after it, killed gliding in competition in the Alps. Of his death Ben wrote, "The tragedy was he died just when his planning gifts were most sorely needed."

Both the photographer and the subject of this photograph that is in the National Portrait Gallery had two brothers who were also at Gresham's, though Ben and Humphrey were not contemporaries at the school. Humphrey was a distinguished photographer. Fifteen of his portraits are in the national collection, including two of his brother, Stephen.

Ben Nicholson wrote in 1930 to Nicolette Gray who was arranging an exhibition in London that included some of his work, saying, "the image can be more actual than the object reflected". He also said in this letter, "*Alice Through the Looking Glass* is among my favourite books". This photograph taken soon afterwards illustrates both these ideas. It also has the same composition as the picture of Ben's that is in it and its fireplace has the same shapes and textures as Ben's abstract pictures of that time. These same ideas are also found in a picture of Ben's in the Kettle's Yard Gallery in Cambridge that he painted in 1930.

His most ambitious picture using reflection is Au Chatte Botte, (Puss in Boots) 1932, that was bought by the Manchester City Art Gallery in 1948. This is a view through a cafe window in Dieppe, with lettering on the inside of the window and reflections from behind him also in the glass. The things in the café are also real in different ways.

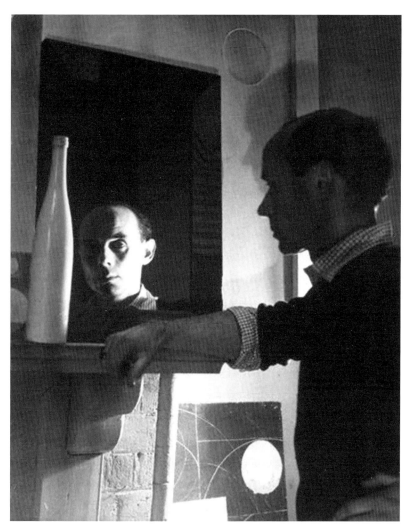

Ben Nicholson by Humphrey Spender (1935)

Tom Wintringham (F 1912-15) was born 1898 in Grimsby. In 1915 he was elected to a Brakenbury scholarship in History at Balliol but postponed his university career to join the Royal Flying Corps. At the end of the war he returned to Oxford, and visited Moscow, after which he returned to England and formed a group of students aiming to establish a British section of the Third International: a Communist Party. In 1923, Wintringham joined the Communist Party of Great Britain, founding the *Daily Worker* in 1930. He

Wintringham in Spain
(Front left in white)

went to Spain as a journalist to cover the Spanish Civil War but joined and eventually commanded the British Battalion of the International Brigades. In 1938, he decided to leave the Communist Party. After Dunkirk in 1940 Wintringham took charge of the Home Guard training school at Osterley Park. His methods were mainly based on his experience in Spain in street fighting and guerilla warfare. After the war he worked in radio and film. While he recognized and opposed the purges of the Soviet Union, he never understood that Stalin himself was responsible for them. Tom Wintringham died on 16 August 1949.

Sir Lennox Berkeley (1903-89, H 1914-18). Berkeley's musical career was heavily influenced by French music. After reading French at Oxford he became a pupil of Nadia Boulanger's in Paris, and worked closely with Ravel. His conversion to Roman Catholicism in 1928 had a significant impact on his work. In 1936 he met Benjamin Britten, who was ten years his junior, and a long and fruitful friendship with him resulted in several collaborative pieces. Lennox Berkeley became Professor of Composition at the Royal Academy of Music and was knighted in 1974.

G. Evelyn Hutchinson (1903-1991, W 1917-21) after Gresham's went to Emmanuel College, Cambridge and then lectured for two years at Witvatersrand Univeristy. He joined the faculty at Yale University in 1928 where he lectured for 43 years and became a US citizen in 1941 where he is known as the founding father of 20th century ecology in the USA. His 4 volume treatise on

Hutchinson and friend

Limnology (1957-93) – the study of the freshwater environment - defined the subject. After his retirement he spent much time in England. He served as the literary executor of Rebecca West. He died in London. The chapter on his time in Woodlands in his autobiography *The Kindly Fruits of the Earth* (Yale University Press, 1979) is a vivid recollection of his time at Gresham's, making clear the astonishing standards and original research in science and the strong influence of Howson and Eccles. He was awarded the National Medal for Science posthumously.

Erskine Hamilton Childers (1905-74, W 1918-24) was born in London. In 1922, when Childers was sixteen, his father was executed by the new Irish Free State. After attending his father's funeral, having promised to shake by the hand everyone who had signed his father's death warrant, Childers returned to Gresham's. After finishing his education, the then Taoiseach of Ireland, Éamon de Valera, invited him back to Ireland to work for the Irish Press. He became a  naturalised Irish citizen in 1938. A member of Fianna Fáil, he held a number of ministerial posts in the cabinets. Childers was elected fourth President of Ireland on 30 May 1973: he proved to be an extremely hard-working president who earned universal respect. Childers's state funeral was attended by world leaders including the Earl Mountbatten of Burma (representing Queen Elizabeth II), the Prime Minister of the United Kingdom, the Leader of the Opposition, and presidents and crowned heads of state from Europe and beyond.

John Hayward (1905-65, W 1918-23) was an important man
of letters, bibliographer and editor
before the war and during the 1950s.
He suffered from muscular dystrophy
and spent most of his adult life in a
wheelchair. He was T. S. Eliot's closest
friend and his flatmate for eleven
years after the war. His proudest claim
was that by his detailed scrutiny and
suggestions he helped to shape *Four
Quartets*. He was awarded the CBE
in 1953 for services to literature and
continued to edit *The Book Collector* until his death.

Robert Medley (1905-94, K 1919-22) was friendly with
Auden at Gresham's and
suggest, to him that he
might write poetry. With
Rupert Doone he founded
the radical Group Theatre
for which he designed
sets for plays by Auden,
Spender and Eliot. After
the thirties he worked as an
official war artist. He was
one of the first British painters to take on abstraction, but his
career spanned the major movements of twentieth century art.
He was awarded the CBE in 1982.

W. H. Auden (1907-73, F 1920-25). Auden wrote an affectionately critical memoir of his schooldays in *The Old School*. After his scientific education at Gresham's Auden went up to Christ Church, Oxford, to read Biology but soon changed to English and established himself as a precociously talented writer. He became the leading poet of his generation, encapsulating the mood and politics of the thirties – that 'low dishonest decade', as he called it. The publication of *Poems* (1930) was a defining moment for twentieth-century British

Auden as a new boy in Farfield (2nd from left in middle row)

poetry. He wrote experimental verse plays for the Group Theatre which was under the direction of his old school friend Robert Medley. After spending the war in America, he became an American citizen in 1946 and his poetry moved away from more overtly political themes as he was converted back to the Christianity of his youth. Auden was also a lecturer, a critic, an essayist and travel writer and collaborated as a librettist with Benjamin Britten. He returned to England and to Oxford University briefly as Professor of Poetry.

Lord Simon of Glaisdale (Jocelyn) (1911-2006 H 1920-25.)

In later life his black eyepatch and bald head made him a cartoonist's dream. After Gresham's he read English at Trinity Hall Cambridge and was later called to the bar serving under Tom, later Lord, Denning. He was made King's Counsel in 1951 and was once described as "That rarity, a reusable ultimate deterrent". In 1951 he also became conservative MP for Middlesborough West. He was under secretary in the Home Office in 1957 and piloted the Homicide Act through the commons with much praise, becoming Solicitor General in 1959. In 1962 he abruptly resigned from politics and became a Judge, specialising in divorce. He was an avowed feminist and secured a divorced wife's right to a share in her husbands pension. He retired in 1977 and served as a crossbencher in the Lords. His Bill there proposing a reform of English spelling was unsuccessful though its proposals are now largely with us through texting.

Bryan, Alan, and David Keith-Lucas

The three **Keith-Lucas brothers** all became professors. Their father had invented the aeronautical compass and **David** (1911-97, W1924-29), the middle brother, was also an aeronautical engineer in a career of twenty-five years for Short Bros and Harland. He pioneered the development of the swept-wing plane which led to his work on the jump jet and was awarded a CBE for his services to the aviation industry. **Alan** (1910-95, W 1922-27) dedicated his life to social work. In order to follow a then nascent profession he made his career in the USA and later became Alumni Distinguished Professor at North Carolina Chapel Hill University. **Bryan** (1912-96, W 1924-30) was a political scientist. After distinguished wartime service, he lectured at Oxford University before becoming Professor of Government at the new University of Kent and then Master of Darwin College, Cambridge. A prominent liberal, he sat on many government committees and, like his brother David, was awarded a CBE.

Sir Christopher Cockerell (1910-99, W 1924-29) was the son
of a museum director and famous
book collector who described him as
no better than a garage hand. After
Gresham's, Christopher Cockerell
read engineering and electronics at
Cambridge, his home town. He then
worked for Marconi and during the
war worked on the first development
of radar which he described as his
most significant achievement. He left
the firm after the war and with his

wife bought a boat hire firm on the Norfolk Broads enabling
him to experiment on his hovercraft designs. Using an empty
Kit Kat tin inside an empty coffee tin, both upside down, he
lifted them with the family vacuum cleaner. Thus the hovercraft
was born and patented in 1955. He also experimented with the
harnessing of wave power to generate electricity and developed
hover trains in the 1970's. It was said he had as many patents
to his name as years when he died, the day after a fly-past to
honour the anniversary of his invention of the hovercraft.

David Lack (1910-73, W 1924-29) was a most distinguished
and original ornithologist. After the war
he became Director of the Edward Grey
Institute at Oxford University. His work
on ornithology was based almost entirely
on the study of the living bird as shown
in his most famous works, *The Life of
the Robin* (1943) and *Darwin's Finches*.
In 1972 he was awarded the Darwin
Medal of the Royal Society.

Professor Sir Alan Hodgkin (1914-98, H 1927-32) read science at Trinity College, Cambridge. He was made a fellow of the college in 1936. After the war he investigated the 'ionic theory of how nerve cells send messages to the brain via an 'electric cable' in the spinal cord and conducted experiments on the nerve fibres of squids and frogs. Sir Alan won the Nobel Prize for medicine in 1963 for 'solving a problem that has haunted physiology for 100 years'. A former President of

the Royal Society, he was knighted in 1972, awarded the Order of Merit the following year and in 1978 became Master of his old college, Trinity, where he was always hospitable to visiting Greshamians. He was a founder of the Trinity Science Park.

Ian Proctor (1918-92, H 1932-37) studied medicine for a while after school but left his studies to join the RAF. After service in air sea rescue in the Mediterranean he was invalided out after suffering from polio, which left him with minor handicaps. He became a Yachting journalist for the Daily Telegraph but mainly he designed yachts with his wife as business manager – the Wayfarer (1958), Single Handed Topper (for beginners) Osprey and

Tempest (this became an Olympic class). His areas of strength were innovative and practical ideas and he pioneered the use of plastics, glass fibre and resins. With Peter Scott he invented the use of the trapeze. He also invented extended aluminum masts – masts produced in his yard have been used in round the world races and the Americas Cup. He died launching a wayfarer.

Peter Pears and Benjamin Britten (on the right)

Benjamin Britten OM (1913-76, F 1928-30) had a precocious talent, composing his first chamber work for strings aged 11. He then began private lessons with Frank Bridge which continued while he was at Gresham's. He wrote 20 works while at school which are still in the repertoire. From school, leaving in the 5ths, he studied at the Royal College of Music. He worked for the GPO film unit 1935-38 where he met W.H. Auden and followed him to USA with Peter Pears. Britten and pears remained there from 1939-42 and when they returned Britten registered as a conscientious objector. His first major success was the opera *Peter Grimes* (1945) followed by many works which built his international reputation, culminating in *The War Requiem*, for the dedication of Coventry Cathedral in 1962. He founded the Aldeburgh festival in 1948 – the Suffolk coast was his spiritual home. The recurring themes of his operas were outsiders misunderstood and loss of innocence.

The cartoonist **Michael Cummings** (1919-97, H 1933-37) was the son of the political editor of the  *New Chronicle* and politics shaped his career as a cartoonist. Beginning on the left-wing journal *Tribune*, he worked on the Daily Chronicle during the war but afterwards became fiercely right-wing. It was with the *Daily Express* under Lord Beaverbrook that the solid black lines of his cartoons became best-known and, to some, notorious. A devoted admirer of Margaret Thatcher, he pilloried those he saw as left-wingers such as Tony Benn and Ted Heath.

Peter Brook (1925- , W 1939-41) is the most influential British theatre director of his time. His  production of *A Midsummer Night's Dream* in 1970 with its set of a lidless white box, trapezes and adult male fairies is a still-remembered landmark production. In the seventies he founded The International Centre for Theatre Research and took its multi-national cast on tours through Africa and Asia. In *The Empty Space* he outlined his views on the importance of theatre and his whole career has been a theatrical odyssey.

Sir Martin Wood FRS (1927- , W [Newquay], 1940-45) once said, "I am a hands on engineer better with my hands than my head." After school he was a Bevin boy in the South Wales and Derbyshire coalfields and then won a Coalboard scholarship to Trinity, Cambridge and Imperial College. He then went to the Clarendon Laboratory and became its Senior Research Officer, 1955-69. Using his knowledge of high magnetic fields based originally on his experiment energising the coil of his car battery he founded

Oxford Instruments which was first located in his garden shed. There he pioneered superconductivity and developed the NMR spectroscope for medical diagnosis and later jointly with Siemans developed the MRI scanner. He has given generously to the Clarendon Laboratory and with his wife has set up trusts to promote nature conservation, forest management and awards for entrepreneurship.

Further Reading

I Will Plant me a Tree, S. G. G. Benson and Martin Crossley Evans, James and James, 2002.

W. H. Auden: a Biography, Humphrey Carpenter, George Allen and Unwin, 1981.

A Schoolmaster's Harvest, J. H. Simpson, Faber and Faber, 1954.

Sane Schooling, J. H. Simpson, Faber and Faber, 1936.

A History of Rendcomb College, C. H. C. Osborne, J. C. James and K. L. James, Rendcomb, 1976.

When Heroes Die, Sue Smart, Breedon Books, 2001.

W. H. Auden and Education, Daniel Varholy, unpublished Oxford D. Phil. Thesis.

INDEX